# UNDER FIRE

## DIARY OF AN ISRAELI COMMANDER
## ON THE BATTLEFIELD

# LT. COL. YONI CHETBOUN

Translated by Jessica Set

gefen
publishing house
JERUSALEM • NEW YORK   Est. 1981

Published in Hebrew by Miskal – Yedioth Ahronoth Books and Chemed Books, 2016

Cover Design: Dragan Bilic – Pixel Droid Design Studio
Typesetting: Raphaël Freeman, Renana Typesetting

ISBN: 978-965-229-916-1

1 3 5 7 9 8 6 4 2

Gefen Publishing House Ltd.
6 Hatzvi Street
Jerusalem 94386, Israel
972-2-538-0247
orders@gefenpublishing.com

Gefen Books
11 Edison Place
Springfield, NJ 07081
516-593-1234
orders@gefenpublishing.com

www.gefenpublishing.com

Printed in Israel

*Library of Congress Cataloging-in-Publication Data*

Names: Chetboun, Yoni, 1979– author. | Setbon, Jessica, translator.
Title: Under fire : diary of an Israeli commander on the battlefield / Yoni
 Chetboun ; translated by Jessica Setbon.
Other titles: Tachat esh. English
Description: Springfield, NJ : Gefen Books ; Jerusalem : Gefen Publishing
 House, [2017]
Identifiers: LCCN 2017014008 | ISBN 9789652299161
Subjects: LCSH: Chetboun, Yoni, 1979---Diaries. | Generals--Israel--Diaries.
 | Lebanon War, 2006--Personal narratives, Israeli.
Classification: LCC DS87.65 .C4413 2017 | DDC 956.9204/5242092--
dc23 LC record available at https://lccn.loc.gov/2017014008

*Dedicated to*
*Beverly and Max Blisko OBM*
*Our dear parents, grandparents and great-grandparents*

צדקה וחסד
קרן משפחת מאיר בליסקא
The Mayer Blisko
Family Foundation

*In memory of my fellow soldiers and commanders
who were killed in battle while fighting for Israel's security,
and with deep love for the bereaved families and the wounded
soldiers of the IDF, who bear their pain on our behalf.*

*For my wife, Ma'ayan*
*Your following Me in the desert, in a land not sown (Jer. 2:2)*

# Contents

# Foreword

During my entire military service in Lebanon, Gaza and Judea and Samaria, I had never seen fog as heavy as that night. A thick cloud covered the Lebanese town, hiding all who approached. In recent years, when I speak about the battle at Bint Jbeil, this is how I describe the fog:

"What's your name?" I ask one of the people in the audience sitting closest to me, just a few feet away. "On that night before the battle began, I wouldn't have been able to see you."

I wrote the first lines of this book out of a need to organize in my mind the chain of events and situations when I was under fire during my military service. Undoubtedly, these were points in time that had a profound influence on my life as a human being, as a husband, and as a father, and later on, as a battalion commander and public representative.

The climax of these events was during the Second Lebanon War.

The writing process brought me back to thoughts and insights I had in battle and over the years. As a commander and officer in the IDF, I had to make on-the-spot decisions, sometimes while under fire. Nothing can compare to this situation. In this book, I have chosen to share these experiences with the reader.

Why does a soldier stand up and charge forward when confronting the enemy? Why do soldiers in battle act in opposition to the natural instinct that is embedded in every human being? What motivates soldiers to overcome fear? What are the qualities that enable an officer to inspire his soldiers with self-confidence and faith in their abilities? These are vital questions that concerned me throughout the writing of this book.

The descriptions of events, thoughts and conclusions that I present here are based on my point of view and personal experiences as an individual and a commander in the IDF. Two people may fight shoulder to shoulder in the exact same battle, but especially when they have different jobs, each will describe the same incident in ways that are different, sometimes drastically. One example of this is the concept of time.

During the battle of Bint Jbeil, I was leading forces through open territory under enemy control, when suddenly shots whizzed past my head. I lay flat on the ground. I don't know how long I lay there before I got up. Was it just a few seconds, or many long minutes? At any rate, I felt that I was laying on the ground for several hours.

The description of events in this book does not attempt to be professional review, nor is it an effort to give complete details of the battle campaigns or about individuals involved. Many of my good friends, the combat soldiers and their officers, carried out acts that were much more important than my own, and had just as much influence on the outcomes of various battles. This is particularly true for the description of the heroic battle at Bint Jbeil, in which dozens of soldiers and officers acted with rare courage and daring to determine the outcome of the battle and achieve victory.

This is not a biography. I do not think that I have done anything so important or significant in my life yet. This is a story about my military service, which integrates insights, thoughts, mistakes, successes, and lessons that can be implemented in civilian life.

This is also the story of a unique decade in the history of the State of Israel, a decade which witnessed the IDF invasion of Lebanon and withdrawal, the outbreak of the Second Intifada, Operation Defensive Shield and the battle against terrorism, the withdrawal from Gaza, the kidnapping of Gilad Shalit, operations in Gaza, and the Second Lebanon War.

Who are the readers for whom I have written this book? Any individual who cherishes the State of Israel will take special interest in the events described here. Such individuals value Israel as a "Zionist preserve," the ultimate expression of Zionism that we all must support, and recognize the importance of the IDF as a people's army that unites all sectors of Israeli society. Israeli youth who are about to be drafted, soldiers and officers of the IDF in regular and reserve service will find this book useful for themselves and their units. Those who are called to the challenge of leadership are invited to confront the dilemmas, the decision-making processes and the choices that accompanied me and my comrades throughout our military service.

\*   \*   \*

My friends, supporters of the State of Israel in the US and around the world: the words and stories to which you will be exposed in this book are the stories of the State of Israel – the state of the Jewish people. My friend and commander Major Roi Klein, of blessed memory, who jumped on a grenade to save his soldiers while shouting *Shema Yisrael,*\* as well as Boaz, Alex, Asaf and other fellow soldiers who were killed in combat, represent the ultimate description of the term "bravery."

As an officer and commander in the IDF, a public representative, and one who is raising his children here in Israel, I call on you to partner with us in continuing to support and strengthen the miracle that is the State of Israel. After 2000 years during which

---

\* *Shema Yisrael* is the pivotal invocation of the Jewish people.

the Jewish people lived in exile, thank God, the State of Israel is blossoming and constantly striding forward. But at the same time, the security challenges it faces have not yet ended. Having served for many years and continuing to serve in the struggle for Israel's security, I am optimistic. I am a firm believer in the basic goodness of humanity and in the amazing powers inherent in the Jewish people in Israel and around the world – powers that will lead to the triumph of good over evil.

This book is dedicated to you in love and true friendship.

# Chapter 1

## Lebanon: The Forgotten Ambush

The first time that I really understood the term "under fire" was when I was actually under fire. I was in the bushes in Lebanon, then a young team leader in the Egoz Special Forces unit, just before the IDF withdrew from Lebanon in 2000. I never dreamed that it would be like this, at least not the first time. I had imagined it differently, much more daring and dynamic, but as the Prussian military theorist Von Clausewitz aptly stated, "War is the realm of uncertainty."*

"Deputy 2, this is Commander. A helicopter's on the way to you. I repeat: a helicopter's on the way to you. There's no way you're staying in the field. Over," Company Commander Roi Klein reports to me.

"Roger, this is Deputy 2. I'm checking out the path to the landing point. I'll update you when we start to move," I replied from the ambush position in the bushes.

The Egoz Special Forces Unit is a commando unit attached to the Northern Command of the IDF. Egoz was identified with the Golani Brigade until 2015, when it was transferred to the Oz

---

* General Carl Philip Gottleib von Clausewitz, *On War.*

1

Commando Brigade. Egoz was reformed in 1995 and designated for operations against the Hezbollah, which aimed to harm IDF soldiers and Israeli citizens.

As a youth, I dreamed of entering an elite IDF unit. I was enchanted by the image of the Egoz fighters, who wore the Golani Brigade badge and operated deep in Lebanese territory. I was the eldest son of immigrants from France who were deeply Zionist. My father served as a flight physician in the reserves, in the Airborne Rescue and Evacuation Unit 669 (heliborne combat search and rescue extraction unit). It was while growing up in my parents' home that I absorbed the ambition for combat service in the IDF.

My dream came true. As a combat soldier in the Egoz unit, in the late 1990s, my military service was replete with operations and ambushes deep in the territory of Southern Lebanon. The main components of our training included helicopter transport, drills on foot in complex landscapes in Northern Israel, and long battle procedures that required learning precise navigation routes at a fine resolution, down to the level of individual bushes on the ground. Physical fitness training sessions along the beach and volleyball games at the unit's base in the north were also an inseparable part of the routine for fighters and commanders alike.

The beginning of the year 2000 marked the eighteenth year of continuous IDF occupation of the security strip in South Lebanon. The media extensively discussed the possibility that the IDF might withdraw from the area. As part of his election campaign, then-Prime Minister Ehud Barak declared his intention to withdraw. Would it happen, and how? When would the new deployment begin? These questions were an unsolved riddle for the Egoz unit, which was entrusted with the job of attacking terror organizations in Lebanon.

We weren't the only ones who were outside the inner circle of information. Despite their disagreement on the topic, Prime Minister Ehud Barak and his chief of staff, Lieutenant General

Shaul Mofaz, preferred not to disclose their discussions about the date of withdrawal, which was planned for July 2000. The two did not even reveal their plans to senior government members or the top military staff, as they feared that the information would be leaked to the media and compromise the surprise factor.

In fact, the date of withdrawal was moved up due to conditions in the field. In May 2000, an agitated Shi'ite mob began to move south, crossing regions that were under the control of the South Lebanon Army (SLA). On the morning of May 24, the SLA began to abandon their posts. There was no force left in the area to stop the marchers and confront them. This was the indicator that led Israel's leaders to order the IDF to withdraw rapidly.

At the time of the IDF's sudden withdrawal from Lebanon, I was a young unit team leader in Egoz, deep inside the bushes in the wadis next to the town of Bint Jbeil in South Lebanon. We were twelve fighters, one squad under team leader First Lieutenant Guy Katz and another squad that I commanded. Our mission was to set ambushes for Hezbollah terrorists going through this area, and eliminate them. Katz's team was completing the unit's training stage. The company commander, Captain Roi Klein, decided that the senior training team should obtain operational experience before completion of the combat track in Egoz.

The plan for the ambush maneuver was to leave from the IDF division post in the town of Bint Jbeil in South Lebanon. We painted our faces in camouflage appropriate for the Lebanese underbrush and soil. After my face was painted brown and green to blend naturally into the environment, I asked to have a photograph taken with my commander, Roi Klein. I had no way of knowing that six years from then, at the beginning of the Second Lebanon War and in that same exact region, the two of us would fight together again.

Team Leader Katz and I went from one soldier to the next, carrying out a careful equipment check to make sure that we had all the weapons on the list. We checked that everything was secure, so that no identifying detail could get left behind in the field. The tiniest thread that fell onto the ground could give away the fact that the IDF had been present – like a sign announcing "Ambush in the area." Leaving equipment in the field was strictly prohibited under all circumstances.

We began to move.

"Yoni, this is Katz, report to me as the last in formation. Over."

The team leader led and I, as sergeant, brought up the rear. Despite our heavy equipment, which included weapons and very large quantities of water and ammunition, the soldiers moved easily through the boulders and underbrush. The branches and trees were twisted and tangled, but the young fighters were excited. They had trained for over a year for just such a mission, and now it was actually happening.

The team leader indicated that we were approaching the deployment point. We went down on our knees and waited for the advance force to survey the area. In past incidents, terrorists had identified our positions while our soldiers were moving, and placed explosive devices on the roads.

"Go ahead, you're clear," reported Katz.

My squad first set up position at a high lookout point. Katz and the force with him slid down to a riverbed and reached their positions in the underbrush. We divided up sections of territory among our squads and performed several training exercises to prepare for encounters with terrorists. Then came the stage that every combat soldier awaited – the sleep shifts.

The waiting period passed calmly and comfortably. The spring weather and hilly landscape, green after the winter rain, had a positive effect. Katz, located at the bottom of the riverbed with the intention of achieving close contact with the terrorists, couldn't make direct contact with the rear operations rooms at the command post. Because I was in a high location, I was the only one who could hear him on the radio and then send a report.

"Yoni, do you hear that?" asked Dotan Gal, waking me. Dotan was the sniper sitting beside me at our unit's position.

The sound of gunfire erupted from fairly close by – single, erratic bursts from the ridge parallel to ours. The team commander asked me to send my report on the shots to the unit command post, to check for changes in our surroundings.

An hour later, the shooting sounded very close to us. Mortar bombs fell and exploded directly above us on the ridge line.

I thought that we had been exposed, and that the enemy had identified our positions. In actuality, a battle of retreat was being waged over our heads between forces of the South Lebanon Army as they abandoned their positions, and the Hezbollah, who seized the opportunity to take control of the area.

Our unit had no idea that the IDF was pulling out of Lebanon.

Had someone in the senior command forgotten the fact that an Egoz team was operating in the field?

Both of our posts prepared for a skirmish. The marksmen and snipers were at the ready, the machine gunners took up their positions, and the lookouts scanned the field. The gunfire came closer and closer, but we had no visual identification of the enemy.

Katz decided to request an evacuation helicopter from the command post. I opened the code map showing the numerical combinations that marked the planned landing spot for the helicopter. Assisting a helicopter landing in complicated conditions and under fire is a basic ability of every fighter in the unit. In almost every exercise, from basic training through battle procedures and operations, we trained to direct and land a helicopter.

"Commander, this is Deputy 2," I contacted the command post. "We need an evacuation helicopter – over."

"Wait!" came the reply from the command post, clearly revealing that there was a problem landing the helicopter. The situation was complex and dangerous. Landing an aircraft at our location was an almost impossible mission. Meanwhile, the mortar bombs and machine gun fire continued to approach.

The communications network blared.

Senior army officials weren't usually heard on the company frequency, but here they were talking on the radio. It was obvious that the IDF, busy with the general retreat, was shaken by the situation of our ambush point. It could easily turn into an adverse international situation.

Suddenly something happened that to my mind triggered the decision to permit the helicopter to enter the area: Company Commander Klein, usually a quiet, straightforward guy, began shouting over the radio at the officer in the command operations room.

"I don't give a damn, do you hear me!?" he screamed, in language that was completely inappropriate for the communications network.

"You're landing that helicopter for them *now*! And I mean *right now*!"

A few minutes later, an officer from the unit command post came on the encrypted network and sent me a new landing coordinate on the code map I held. I noted that the new coordinate was about 1.8 miles (3 km) south of our position. We then had to plan the appropriate navigational course for this maneuver, to avoid exposing ourselves to enemy fire.

As the team leader was down in the wadi and could not hear what was going on at the unit command post, I updated him about the landing of the Owl helicopter for rescue at the new point, and instructed him to begin packing up the equipment.

We moved southward rapidly. The thick Lebanese underbrush and massive boulders made movement very difficult. Our breathing intensified due to the effort of carrying heavy equipment on our backs. The helicopter landed just as we arrived at the landing point, and we realized that it couldn't wait on the ground for more than a few seconds – it was too dangerous.

The helicopter rotor pushed the air at us in waves, slowing our progress. The helicopter door opened. Commander Katz sat next to the pilot's cabin to plan the navigation route back. I, the sergeant, stood outside the door according to procedure, and counted the fighters as they rushed inside.

1, 2, 3.. 11.

One was missing.

In that crazy situation, the last thing we needed now was to lose a soldier or leave one in the field.

"The dog trainer from Oketz is missing!" the soldiers shouted at me from the belly of the helicopter.

Oketz is the IDF's outstanding K-9 unit that trains dogs for a number of operational uses, such as identification of explosive material, tracking, attack, and search and rescue. The dog handlers undergo an intensive and particularly challenging training course. Attack dogs that are able to identify, attack and neutralize terrorists are particularly efficient in the complex territory of Lebanon. I don't envy the terrorist who becomes the target of an Oketz dog.

A dog handler and an attack dog had been with us at our ambush position, but now as we entered the helicopter, we couldn't find him.

"There you are! Where did you disappear to? Get inside!" I shouted over the din of the helicopter's rotors.

"The dog's afraid of the noise! He keeps trying to run away," the dog handler updated me.

"Hey, isn't he supposed to be trained for this noise?" I replied. "He can stay here for all I care." This was a serious insult to an Oketz guy, as the dogs of their unit are considered to be combat soldiers in every sense of the term, and to leave one in the field was tantamount to abandoning a human soldier in enemy territory.

The helicopter technician informed me over the radio that if we didn't take off in another second, we ran a serious risk of direct and immediate fire. The stubborn dog handler wouldn't give in. He grabbed the dog firmly in his powerful arms and climbed into the helicopter.

It was relatively quiet as we flew over Lebanese territory. In the darkness, we could barely make out the white lights of the villages of South Lebanon and the roads leading to the town of Bint Jbeil. After crossing the border into Israel, we turned west and the helicopter flew down the northern coastline on its way to the landing strip at the unit's base.

From the helicopter window, I saw strange yellow lights shining down the length of the coast and in the open spaces of territory between settlements in the north. I pushed closer to the window to get a better look, puzzled at this strange sight. Then I remembered – that night was Lag Ba'Omer, a holiday when the Jews traditionally light bonfires. The hundreds of bonfires lit by youths, families and kids indicated that in Israel, life continued as usual.

Lag Ba'Omer also marks the period of the Bar Kochba rebellion against the cruel Roman regime after the destruction of the Second Temple. In a fraction of a second before we began the landing process, I was able to reflect on the fact that in contrast to Bar Kochba's fighters, I was proudly wearing the uniform of the Defense Forces of the State of Israel. At the same time, I couldn't ignore the fact that the reason we were in a helicopter was because our army had withdrawn.

At the landing strip, senior members of our unit were waiting to greet us, bearing trays of grapes and sweet drinks. We conducted a preliminary equipment check.

"We have to remember to thank Company Commander Klein. It's thanks to him that we're here." I felt a particular need to share this thought with the other soldiers.

* * *

Rosh Chodesh Av 5772 (2012) on Mt. Herzl. This was the date of the annual memorial ceremony honoring Major Roi Klein, deputy commander of Battalion 51, who was killed in the Second Lebanon War. I stood, embarrassed, in front of dozens of people who had come to honor my friend and commander Roi. In a few minutes, it would be my turn to speak. Sara, Roi's wife, had asked me two days previously to say a few words in his honor. The night before the memorial ceremony, I tried to record some memories and thoughts from the long period of army service that I had shared with Klein. But the letters and words wouldn't come together on paper – it just didn't work. I decided that the next day I would speak off the cuff.

"I would like to share with you a story about closing a loop, or actually, a loop that was never really closed."

The words came out of my mouth spontaneously, as I hadn't prepared a written speech. I began to tell the story of the operation at Bint Jbeil that preceded the IDF's withdrawal from Lebanon. That moment on Mt. Herzl, six years after the war, was the first time that I had ever told Klein's family about his commitment to getting us out back in the year 2000.

I continued. "In 2006, during the Second Lebanon War, again deep inside Bint Jbeil, I very much wanted to close that loop and repay Roi by saving his life as he had saved mine. But sadly, I wasn't able to get Roi out alive, and so I wasn't able to thank him for what he did for me."

I looked over at his parents, Shoshi and Aharon, and at his wife Sara and the kids, and said, "Thank you."

## HANITA AMBUSH?

The soldiers on Katz's team completed their training and joined another company in Egoz, while I went back to my position as a regular member of A Company.

The period following the IDF's withdrawal from South Lebanon was very complicated for Egoz Unit. Uncertainty permeated the atmosphere, and questions peppered the conversations of commanders and fighters alike: What was the purpose of Egoz Unit? Did Egoz still have a reason to exist? Ambush missions like the ones we carried out in the past, in which we had penetrated deep into Lebanon, were no longer relevant, and this led us to a feeling of inactivity and irrelevance.

One day, Tal, the team commander, informed me, "We're going on an ambush in Kibbutz Hanita."

"Where?" we asked. For a minute, we thought he was joking.

"Yes, Hanita. The region is full of undergrowth and close to the border, and there's a risk that the Hezbollah will exploit the new situation and try to attack the kibbutz, which is near the fence."

As fighters, we weren't really interested in his analysis of the situation. For us, an ordinary march of a few hundred yards through the Hanita riverbed inside Israeli territory made us feel like the big guys were just trying to find something for us to do. Of course we went through with the "ambush" at Hanita and similar operations during that period, but without great enthusiasm.

\* \* \*

Later during my military service as a commander, and further on in life as a member of Knesset, the words "Hanita Ambush" took on a formative meaning for me. In the military, as well as in public life, there are many acts and concepts that may seem dull and insignificant. I have learned, however, that these thoughts and deeds are a significant and vital component in the life of a state. This understanding is a basic requirement for anyone who has chosen to serve his nation. The aspiration to rise above the grayness of ordinary service, to act and to inspire others around you to perform every task required in the best possible manner, is an inseparable part of the task of anyone who chooses to participate in military, educational or public leadership.

I am hardly revealing a big secret here. The life of a combat soldier is not filled with daily encounters with terrorists. Most of the time, an ordinary soldier will hear the command "Attack!" only in training exercises. The rest of the time passes in endless hours of guard duty on freezing winter nights, infinite patrols along borders, and boring stakeouts. Yet these activities are a central component in the routine maintenance of the security of the State of Israel. As part of this vital component, hundreds of hostile terrorist incidents are prevented thanks to open or secret activities by the IDF and other security forces. A commander at any level who does not understand the crucial significance of leading routine security activity would be better off looking for another profession.

## Chapter 2

# My First Encounter as Egoz Team Leader

"Chetboun, report to the company commander's office," Team Leader Tal informs me. The command caught me in the middle of a challenging game of volleyball in my company's courtyard at the Egoz unit base.

"You're starting the officers' training course. Preparation begins in two weeks. Good luck," announced our company commander, Captain David Zini, without asking me.

I was a real gung-ho soldier, and in the past I had seriously considered becoming an officer, as I had been brought up with that goal. But in that uncertain period, the officers' training course wasn't the first thing on my personal list of priorities, especially when my fast-approaching release date was looking more tempting than ever.

But after less than twenty-four hours of deliberation, my conscience wouldn't permit me to refuse. I gave a positive reply, along with three friends who were also considering the same option. We all knew that we wouldn't necessarily return to command positions in our unit. In the optimal scenario, we would be sent to one of the brigades in the Golani division, and in the less preferable case, we would be sent out of the Golani division.

The officers' training course at Bahad 1 training base and the encounter with individuals of outstanding quality in Israeli society are amazing experiences. The course I underwent, which began in October 2000, was particularly unique. As cadets, we were exposed to a new period in the history of the State of Israel, which eventually became known as the Second Intifada.

On Rosh Hashanah 5760, during one of the meals in my family's home, I received an unusual phone call informing me that we wouldn't be spending the course in the usual classrooms of Bahad 1 training base in the south.

"Come to Arlozorov station today at seven p.m. Apparently, we're being sent to Gaza," said Asaf, a fellow cadet of the course.

The members of the Gefen battalion spent the next few weeks at Kissufim post on the border of the Gaza Strip. Battle procedures for ambushes, patrols and operations in the region became part of the program, in on-the-job training style.

At the beginning of the twenty-first century, cities and towns in Israel became targets for lethal terrorist attacks. Suicide bombings by terrorists wearing explosive belts became a routine occurrence. Driving on the roads of Judea and Samaria became highly dangerous for families who lived there, and still do today. The faces of soldiers and civilians whose lives were cut off in the previous day's attacks stared out at us from the front pages of the morning newspapers.

On October 12, 2000, we heard over the post radio about the lynch and murder of reserve soldiers Yossi Avrahami and Vadim Nurzhits in Ramallah by a rioting Arab mob. Photos showing the distorted faces of the murderers, their hands dripping with blood, became the recognized symbol of the Second Intifada. At the time, the course participants were twenty-year-old cadets representing the entire range of Israeli politics. At night, we argued vociferously about the future of the country that we loved so much, and about possible solutions for the Arab-Israeli problem. The lynch in Ramallah changed everything. Now everyone realized that we had to destroy Islamic terror, and that this was a cruel war of ideologies.

The seven months of the challenging and intensive officers' training course transformed us into a unified group. The individuals that made up Team 16, under the command of First Lieutenant Reuven Hazoni, exemplified the fascinating variety of Israeli society. Doron from Kibbutz Mizra, Kasulara from Arad, Yaron from Beit El, and Dolev from Petach Tikva were just some of the future officers of the people's army, and their common denominator was Zionist values and love for the Land of Israel.

As commanders of companies of young soldiers in the future, we realized that the morning after the course was over, our lives would certainly not be any easier, particularly during this period of intifada. On the last night before the promotion ceremony, I chose this verse from the Book of Isaiah and printed it out in tiny letters: "For the sake of Zion I will not be silent, and for the sake of Jerusalem I will not rest, until her righteousness shines out like brilliance, and her salvation burns like a torch" (62:1). I folded the slip of paper into four and pushed it into the ID tag pouch that I wore next to my chest. The words had special meaning for me then, and they still do today. To me they symbolize the essence of Zionism, and the commitment of each and every one of us to participate actively in the continued existence and success of the State of Israel, as the previous generations did.

Thirteen years later, when I became a member of the Israeli Knesset, I made my own commitment to upholding those same powerful words. In my first address to the Knesset in 2013, I opened that yellowed slip of paper for the first time, and read the words to my fellow Knesset members. This time I was wearing a new suit and a button-front shirt instead of my army uniform. Despite the negative image that politics has in society, it must attract young, talented individuals from all sectors of society, who are willing to take responsibility for realizing the Zionist vision in the decision-making space in the Knesset and the Israeli government.

The transformation of youth into combat soldiers in the Israel Defense Forces is a fascinating challenge that combines military professionality and educational messages. Every Friday, "Yoni's Team," the group with which I began my term of service as a team leader, was obligated to hear a selection from the collected letters of another Yoni – Yoni Netanyahu.

My parents made aliya (immigrated) from France. To them, as for many others throughout the Jewish world, Yoni Netanyahu and the heroic Entebbe rescue operation was the ultimate symbol of Israeli heroism. As their eldest son born shortly after their aliya, they gave me the name Yoni, after the Entebbe hero.

As a youth, I devoured descriptions, articles and books about Lt. Yoni Netanyahu. When I became an officer in the IDF, I felt the need to convey his image to my cadets, who didn't always understand why I was pestering them.

The period in which I trained combat soldiers as a team leader passed rapidly, and soon I was called up to command an operational team in A Company in the Egoz Unit. The operational company commanders were busy round-the-clock in battle against terror organizations. Under the command of Lieutenant Colonel Tamir Yadai, Egoz Unit quickly adapted itself to the new reality and led successful operations in Gaza and Judea and Samaria. Its skills of camouflage, assimilation into the field, and guerrilla warfare tactics that it acquired over the years of battle in Lebanon proved efficient in battle against Hamas and Fatah terrorists as well.

"Hi, my name is Yoni, and we're going to be together for a while," I announced at the first meeting with the team of fighters now under my command. I gave this introductory talk a few minutes before the Operational Group 1 briefing that preceded an ambush operation in the sand dunes of the Gaza Strip. If I had thought that I would have time to learn to be a team leader, I was very wrong.

The fifteen fighters were crowded into a small room to meet their new team leader, and they were too tired to listen to a lengthy acquaintance speech. "In twenty minutes be in uniform and at the briefing room to receive your orders," I continued, realizing that they had no time or patience for manners.

Stern, a soldier in the team who knew me from before, advised me warmly, "Don't bug them too much. Loosen up a little, it's not easy around here."

In the coming months, Stern's advice took on added significance, as I regularly confronted differences of opinion about discipline and military organization. The challenging operational activities, the difficulties and successes in battle, including Operation Defensive Shield, eventually led to a productive, friendly balance between myself and the team.

## ATTACK ON ASKAR CAMP

The IDF units developed various techniques for inducing armed terrorists hiding in inhabited areas to expose themselves, and thus become the target of IDF fire that awaited them. Such operations were called "stimulated response." These operations were a significant component of the efforts the IDF invested in the war on terror in the early twenty-first century.

The team under my command was given the mission of implementing a stimulated response at the Askar camp. This camp is actually an eastern suburb of the city of Nablus (Shechem), and it is divided into "Old" and "New" Askar. The method was simple but daring. We planned to leave from the "Pita" post, located at the entrance to the settlement of Alon Moreh, advance covertly on foot, cross the village of Azmut, and set up an ambush at the edge of the inhabited area of the two Askar camps. A tank force that was coordinated with us planned to enter the camp and lure the terrorists out into the alleys of the camp and expose themselves.

The success of the operation depended on secrecy, surprise and rapid disconnection after performing the mission. But as often happens in the reality of battle, plans remain just that – plans. In the field, things take place a bit differently.

As a team leader, I was very worried about crossing the village of Azmut on the way to the target. Premature exposure would mean we would not surprise the terrorists at Askar. Colonel Yossi Adiri, commander of the Samaria brigade, solved the dilemma for me in a simply manner: "Chetboun, if you meet any terrorists on the way – that will be a success in and of itself. Just make sure they don't go home alive."

Half an hour before departure, we "smoked" our uniforms and equipment around a small bonfire. Exposing these items to smoke limits the odor of bodies and sweat and thus reduces the chances that dogs will bark at us. Any IDF recruit who has navigated through Southern Israel during military service knows the uncomfortable feeling of dogs barking when soldiers approach Bedouin tents in the darkness of night. I perform the departure check and give each soldier a number for count-off. Then we begin to advance on foot along the dry riverbed leading to the village. As team leader, I had the feeling that this time we would make contact. Nablus was teeming with terrorists, and chances were high that this time we would run into them.

I led the advance team, which was composed of top-notch fighters, at a short distance from the rest of the force. On my right was Alnakri the machine gunner, on my left was Vaknin, marksman and navigator, and behind me came Matof the signaler, who was armed with grenade launchers.* The goal of the advance team

---

* An M-203 grenade launcher, a weapon that shoots grenades at a range of several hundred yards.

was to carry out stops for efficient observation into new sections of territory, to navigate, and to be ready to encounter the enemy in a more flexible manner than the rest of the force.

We continued to advance down the wadi toward Azmut. We stopped for observation. Everything looked closer and more tangible.

The village was dark and sleepy, but the approach road was illuminated with powerful lights. There was no other way forward – we had to cross the road. Over the radio, I ask the brigade observation posts to scan the village and the road crossing point.

"Clean. No identification of movement. Good luck."

I knew that at those moments there are numerous people at the operation command post who are waiting for this stage to be completed successfully, and I felt the weight of responsibility.

Two by two, the fighters crossed the road rapidly and crept silently along the southern edge of the village. We advanced close to the houses. I was calm and conveyed a sense of confidence to the soldiers, as we had already passed the most complex section of the approach to the target.

But in the next few minutes, this assumption was disproved.

We climbed up a cliff with houses on top that marked the western edge of Askar camp. Company Commander Roi Klein spoke on the radio with the commander of the tank force and prepared him for the fact that we were approaching the target. We were almost on top. I announced a stop to drink. The climb was not easy and we had to conserve our strength for the mission. The experienced fighters drank one after another, so that there were always marksmen and lookouts from within the group to scan the territory.

"Stop!" Vaknin declared, placing his hand on my shoulder, while he continued to look through the night vision equipment that was attached to his weapon.

"What's going on?" I whispered.

"Look toward the road," he replied. I lifted the night vision equipment and looked inside.

"Dammit! They identified our crossing."

Some 450 yards away, a white car was parked on the road. Three men got out of the car and placed an explosive device on the road to Azmut village. They had identified our crossing and planned to blow us up when we were on our way back.

"Hold your fire!" I order over the radio.

The weapons we were carrying would not be effective over a distance of 450 meters, and inexact fire would not harm the terrorists – it would only drive them away. We had to make contact with them. Time was running out.

After consulting with the company commander, I place a covering force consisting of a machine gunner and marksman on a high point, and set out on an outflanking maneuver, aiming to open fire on the terrorists and attack.

I decide to move southward on a concealed route at the base of Azmut riverbed, and then cut east toward the terrorists and surprise them. Everything was fast and very close. I moved rapidly with the advance team and another squad. The southern end of the riverbed is muddy and full of water. The winter of 2002 was blessed with copious rainfall, but that didn't help us at all.

I jumped into the riverbed and began to cross. "There's no way that those beasts are getting away from us," I mutter to myself.

My legs felt heavy and I began to sink. This section of the riverbed was a swamp. The advance team pulled me out, saving me from an unplanned drowning. The difficulty only intensified my desire to complete the mission.

"Yoni, this is Sifroni," reported the team fighter at the observation post. "The scumbags are starting to pack up their equipment and put it back in the car. In a minute they'll be gone," reported the team member at the observation post.

I gave the prearranged signal for a sudden ambush. The firing angle was terrible, but we had no other choice. We spread out rapidly in a line. I was proud of the combatants, as this was exactly what we had learned: "In battle as in training."

I began the countdown: "Prepare to fire, 7..6.., 2..1, fire!"

What was going on down there? I had to get a status report.

It looked like two terrorists were wounded, and they were dragging the body of the third terrorist into the car. They started the car and began to drive.

"Launch a grenade!"

The grenade exploded close to the terrorists, and the car raced off toward Nablus and disappeared into the city. Adrenalin continued to pump through my body. Aside from the fact that we had clearly done our best under the conditions, I had a vague feeling of missed opportunity. That's the way it is in battle.

I verify the count-off numbers over the radio. Everyone was present, there were no wounded.

Forward march! We had to move back to the post.

The cover squad joined us, and in coordination with the observation squad we choose a crossing point at a distance, in order to avoid getting dangerously close to the explosive device that the terrorists had planted.

At Samaria Brigade headquarters, the cook had prepared us a hot and tasty post-mission feast. We got organized for the equipment check and preliminary mission review.

It was 4:00 a.m., and I sent a message to Ma'ayan: "We're back. All is well, Yoni." At that time, Ma'ayan and I had just begun to go out, and at that early stage in our relationship I already felt that she was the one I would marry.

Sergeant Yossi, whose father worked in the security forces, informed us gleefully that the Palestinians were reporting one dead and one wounded who was admitted to the Nablus hospital after an encounter with the IDF.

Two days later was the mission review at unit headquarters in the north. The unit commander was busy on another operation in Gaza, so his subordinate, Major Rafi Milo, carried out the review instead. Rafi had been commander of the Shayetet, the naval commando unit, and he was thorough and to the point. While praising the team's conduct during the encounter, he did not spare me criticism over the fact that we hadn't liquidated all of the terrorists. As usual, Company Commander Klein backed me up. He told Rafi about our attempt to make contact and how I had almost drowned while crossing the riverbed.

We didn't have too long to digest these events, as one week after my first encounter as an officer and commander, I found myself in the Gaza Strip and on the Rafiah border, carrying out arrests, raids and ambushes along with the other fighters on the team.

*   *   *

As an officer, the experience of encountering the enemy was vastly different from that same experience as a soldier. A commander under fire, or in contact with the enemy, has to draw upon powerful resources and reserves of strength. In a flash, I realized that all the responsibility fell on my shoulders. Hesitation, freezing in place or inability to function could have caused loss of life, and would have thwarted the goal. In the reality of battle in the IDF, these failures meant harming the lives of citizens.

Throughout all of military history, the issue of soldiers charging in the line of fire has interested many, commanders and researchers alike. What motivates a soldier to get up from his hiding place and run into fire? This act would seem to contradict basic human instinct. The range of answers to this question is very wide. Some assert that the soldier's feeling of shame is the main motivation for the charge and accompanying risk, but I disagree with this theory. Throughout my battle experience, alongside demonstrations of extraordinary bravery and courage I also witnessed soldiers who were afraid, who remained behind and watched as their comrades endangered their lives. The soldiers who behaved this way were few but, still, they were present.

Anyone who has experienced such moments knows that there are two basic components that motivate a soldier to get up and place himself in danger. The first component is the values that he has learned. Identification with the importance of the moment and the mission is an expression of the moral foundations that he inherits in his parents' home, in the educational institutions he has attended and the youth movements where he absorbed fundamental concepts. In certain rare cases, the soldier acquires these values – dedication, responsibility, love of land and country – during his military service.

Here I would like to emphasize that when the values of friendship and social cohesion are well entrenched in a military unit, they will serve to amplify a soldier's fighting power when he is asked to endanger himself in an attack. Friendship is not the soldier's feeling of shame in front of his friends, but rather a value in and of itself, which motivates fighters to get up and take action. The Israeli army also serves as a greenhouse for the development of Zionist values among the youth of our nation. To my way of thinking, the act of donning olive drab itself develops a sense of moral obligation in the soldier.

The second component is the soldier's trust in his commander. The image of the commander who must lead his soldiers on the battlefield is a crucial factor. A commander who has mastered the military discipline and has the appropriate decision-making ability enables his subordinates to trust him even when under fire. Aside from the ethical component, the commander's professionality in operating weapons, moving forces, orientation in the field, and navigation permits the soldier to carry out acts that are liable to place him in significant danger.

The trust about which I am speaking is not built for the subordinate only at the endpoint when facing the enemy. At the lowest level of command, beginning with squad commander and ending with company commander, the commander gains his soldiers' trust in a gradual process. In fact, the commander of forces in the field is tested by his subordinates twenty-four hours a day. The friction between them is constant and intense. The smallest details take on great importance: how he stands in front of them, the tone of his voice, the look in his eyes, how he slaps them on the shoulder. These are just as important as his physical strength and his leadership in the drills, weapons training and marches.

The soldiers who choose to join the officers' training courses in field units and in the general military deserve to be praised by their commanders and by all of society. At the same time, every commander must recognize the weight of responsibility that rests on his shoulders from the moment he accepts his command. The work of commanding requires both leadership and professional skill. The commander must study himself in the mirror every day. He must examine himself honestly in order to prove that he is carrying out his job correctly, both as a commander and as a professional.

## OPERATION DEFENSIVE SHIELD: IN ARAFAT'S OFFICE

As a young team leader at the far end of the command chain, I felt a sense of success during the wave of arrests and complex mission that the Egoz Unit soldiers performed along with the other combat forces. But in broader perspective, the operational and political reality was not so rosy.

Between 2000 and 2002, the IDF and other security forces adopted a policy of "containment," using force in reaction to incidents and without initiating. In 2001 alone, 247 soldiers and civilians were killed or murdered, and 2,594 were wounded. In 2002, the slaughter intensified, and 453 Israelis were killed, of whom 295 were civilians.*

---

\* Data from Brigadier General Oren Avman, *Zarkor Histori* [Spotlight on History: The War on Palestinian Terror].

Entrance on foot into the territory governed by the Palestinian Authority (Area "A") was considered exceptional and against the normal operating procedures. The attitude that reigned in the senior levels of command was to prevent any change in the status quo. This meant exercising restraint in order to avoid escalation. Against the background of the wave of terror, in February 2001 Ariel Sharon defeated Ehud Barak in the direct elections for prime minister. But the elections did not precipitate any significant change in policy in relation to the Palestinian Authority and its leader, Yasser Arafat.

On the wall above the bunk bed in the officer's room at my unit, I hung up photos of the civilians who were murdered on an almost daily basis and whose faces stared out from the front pages of the newspapers. First Lieutenant Boaz Pomerantz, a quiet, professional team leader from Kiryat Shemona, slept in the bunk underneath me. In the crazy race from battle procedures to missions, Boaz and I managed to talk about our personal lives, the weddings and the big trip abroad we planned to take after finishing the army. We talked about many other topics as well, and once we even had a discussion on the definition of the word "Zionism."

The mosaic of commanders in Company A also included Safi, a Druze team leader, who stood out for his exceptional daring and exemplary dedication to his soldiers. Roi Klein, the company commander, was about to finish in his position, soon to be replaced by Major Udi Ben Hamu.

Home leave was a rare occurrence during that period. On weekends when we were allowed time off, I took advantage of the time to see Ma'ayan. Our relationship began with a chance meeting at an optician's shop between my mother, who worked in the store, and her Aunt Nicole. This meeting led to our acquaintance. As the Sages say, "Matches are made forty days before the fetus is created" – and in our case, this proved accurate, as after just eight meetings including a long weekend that was cut short, we decided to get engaged.

I arrived at the henna ceremony, which is a tradition in our family, about fifteen minutes late, after a successful arrest operation in the Sebastia region of Samaria. I entered the event hall wearing a uniform that reeked of sweat, with camouflage paint still on my face – somewhat embarrassed, but thrilled.

The wedding date was set for the week before Passover 5762 (March 2002). Ma'ayan took care of all the arrangements with the assistance of our families, from the hall to the food, the band, the guest list and the invitations. As a team leader in the early twenty-first century, we were busy every night with arresting terrorists who were planning an attack for the next day, and getting married seemed like a privilege. Even my suit and other clothes were chosen and bought by my parents, in the hopes that the sizes were correct.

Ma'ayan and I worried that the date of the wedding might be a problem for our families and guests, as they would be busy with Passover cleaning and preparations. We never anticipated that Ma'ayan would spend the holiday alone in our new home, while I was deep in the city of Ramallah, just four yards from Chairman Yasser Arafat's office.

In February 2002, government and military policy began to change. Two successful and simultaneous infantry operations gave the decision-makers confidence that it was possible and even preferable to enter cities that were inside the Palestinian Authority. The Golani Brigade entered the so-called "refugee camp" in Jenin, and at the same time the Paratrooper Brigade attacked Balata camp in Nablus. During a course for battalion commanders in the reserves, Oren Abman, then commander of battalion 12 of Golani Brigade (today Brigadier General) shared with us an indication of his feelings just before the attack on Jenin. Abman had asked the adjutant and the battalion's rabbi whether the truck for removing bodies was prepared, and whether there were enough body bags on hand for the casualties expected as a result of this operation. The positive results of the infantry operations surprised everyone.

During the Golani operation in Jenin, under the command of Colonel Chico Tamir, 137 terrorists were wounded. Colonel Aviv Kochavi, commander of the Paratrooper Brigade, summarized the results at a press conference held at a lookout near Nablus: "The tiger of Balata turned out to be a kitten."

"Yoni, prepare and learn the navigation route. Your team will lead the brigade. Tomorrow night we're going into Ramallah," said Major Udi Ben Hamu, the new company commander.

After the terror attack on Moment Café in Jerusalem, in which eleven civilians were killed and fifty-eight injured, Chief of Staff Shaul Mofaz decided to carry out an operation to put pressure on Arafat's headquarters. In the briefing at Judea and Samaria division headquarters, near Beit El, the highlights emphasized were already familiar to us from our unit commanders: "You must be emotionally prepared for injuries. The battle will take place in a very complex inhabited area."

The infantry operation began. A long line of combatants marched behind me in the dead of night. We moved at a level about two-thirds up the ridge, with the city's modern buildings visible above us. I approached the target and reported this to Udi on the radio. We crouch down in place, and the lookouts report quiet in the area, with little movement in the city. We waited about half an hour for approval to attack, with the winter cold penetrating our bones.

"Commander to One, accept a change in mission. We're going back to the base. Over," Udi reports.

"This is One. Roger," I replied, realizing that someone higher up had got cold feet. The visit of General Anthony Zinni (Ret.), the American envoy to Israel and the Palestinian Authority, led the decision-makers to withdraw all Israeli forces from Area A.

\*   \*   \*

Our wedding day arrived. I took a day off and even managed to try on the suit my parents had bought for me. Because of the security situation, Ma'ayan and I were aware that many guests were afraid to come out to the hall, which was at Kibbutz Zir'a near Beit Shemesh. Just three days earlier, terrorists had carried out an attack on Road 38, which led to the kibbutz. But we were pleasantly surprised – the hall was chock full, and we even had more guests than we had invited. This is the genetics of Israeli society – happy occasions, and especially during difficult security situation, bring people out of their homes.

The guests danced to the official brigade song "Golani, My Golani," and waved the Israeli flag and the brigade flag. My friends from the unit and the rest of my military service surprised me by arriving and celebrating along with us. Rabbi Avichai Rontzki, who later became chief rabbi of the IDF, performed the wedding ceremony. Standing under the *chuppah*, I choked back my tears as I read the prayer for the welfare of the IDF soldiers and the security forces:

> He who has blessed our forefathers, Abraham, Isaac and Jacob – may He bless the soldiers of the Israel Defense Forces and the members of the security forces, who stand guard over our land and the cities of our God, from the border of Lebanon to the Egyptian desert, and from the Mediterranean Sea to the approach of the Arava, on land, in the air, and by sea.
>
> May the Almighty cause the enemies who rise up against us to be struck down before them. May the Holy One, Blessed is He, preserve and rescue our fighters from every trouble and distress, and from every plague and illness, and may He send blessing and success in their every endeavor.
>
> May He lead our enemies under our soldiers' sway, and may He grant them salvation and crown them with victory.
>
> And may there be fulfilled for them the verse: "For it is the Lord your God, Who goes with you to battle your enemies for you to save you."

Years afterward, I still meet people who tell me that they were very moved by the joyful atmosphere at our wedding, which took place during an extremely tense and painful time. At every wedding that I attend, I always feel a special sense of renewed life and hope. The feeling of *am Yisrael chai* – "the nation of Israel lives," may seem banal in ordinary times, especially to the generation that grew up here in Israel. But at weddings it takes on a powerful dimension. Today, more than ever, I feel that the foundation for our continued existence as a people rests on strengthening Jewish family values.

Seder night in 5762 (2002) was the night that my new wife Ma'ayan and I were supposed to finish the *sheva berachot*, a week of festive dinners for the newlyweds held after the wedding. We were guests at the home of family in Moshav Ahuzam near Kiryat Gat. "May the Lord, our God and God of our forefathers, enable us to attain other holidays and festivals in the future in peace, rejoicing in the rebuilding of Your city and delighting in Your service ... Blessed are You, God, Redeemer of Israel." With these words, we concluded the first portion of the Haggadah, before beginning Shulchan Orech, the festive meal. The table was spread with a bounty of special Passover foods in the Moroccan tradition.

Rafi, an uncle who lived nearby, walked in the door, which had been left open for Elijah the Prophet, wearing a serious expression. He didn't look like he was bringing good news.

"There was a big terror attack in Netanya."

The guests, including my close family and myself who were Netanya residents, jumped from their chairs.

"Where exactly?" we asked.

"The Park Hotel. Dozens were killed and wounded," he continued. "The news reported a terrorist went into the big Seder held at the hotel and blew himself up inside."

Despite the painful news, we continued with the Seder meal and recited the Haggadah, as we were celebrating the holiday of freedom. Still, a small voice inside me whispered that I could no longer be sure that I would celebrate my first holiday as a married man together with my wife. I checked my cellphone – no call yet from my unit.

The neighbors had their television on, and they reported nineteen dead and dozens of wounded. Later the toll grew to thirty dead and 160 wounded, including married couples and families with children who had come to the hotel to celebrate Seder night together. The attack on the Park Hotel changed the military reality and policy in Judea and Samaria, and led to a change in government policy and awakening from the deep sleep of the Oslo agreements.

We went to bed, and I placed my cellphone next to me. Despite the fact that this was a festival and using a phone was in principle forbidden according to Jewish law, saving a life took precedent. In the security situation of the twenty-first century, I instructed all of my soldiers, whether or not they abided by Jewish law, to carry their cellphones twenty-four hours a day, seven days a week, including Shabbat and holidays, and to be constantly prepared for call-up.

"Yoni, your phone's ringing," murmured Ma'ayan at 2:00 a.m.

The name Boaz Pomerantz appeared on the screen.

"Yeah, bro," I answered.

"Listen, we're preparing for a serious operation. Udi the company commander just called me. Inform your team quickly to report to the transport stations in Haifa, Tel Aviv, Jerusalem and Be'er Sheva tomorrow at 8:00 a.m. Talk to you later…"

Just two days later, Boaz was killed on a staircase in a building next to where I was, at the beginning of the attack on Ramallah. A terrorist waiting in the upper section of the building shot him, and was in turn immediately killed by Boaz's soldiers.

Throughout my military service, Ma'ayan and I often had to cut short vacation, change personal plans, or say a hasty goodbye on the phone, due to urgent military operations, when my unit was sent into enemy territory or even war. Understandably, in the months when we were dating and during our engagement, we both became fans of Yankele Rothblit's song "*Lo kala darkeinu*" – "Our path isn't easy," which perfectly described the period in which we chose to start our family.

The morning of the first day of Passover 2002 was the first time I said goodbye to Ma'ayan as a married man. Looking back at that time, neither of us really understood the significance of that goodbye. Later, after we were a family with children and more experienced in the ways of battle, these goodbyes became more difficult. I often say that military couples have special strengths that enable them to overcome this challenge. But at the time, just one week after the wedding, we were real greenhorns.

In the morning my father places his palm on my head and gives me his blessing: "May the Lord bless you and keep you. May the Lord shine His face upon you and be gracious to you. May the Lord lift up His countenance upon you and grant you peace." My grandmother asks me to place my hand on the *mezuzah*, and she recites a silent blessing. After kissing my worried family, my cousin Dan drives me to the central bus station in Be'er Sheva.

That Passover, the roads to the unit base in the north were packed with buses full of soldiers, enlisted men and reserves, who had been called up for emergency service. Later, when I was a member of Knesset, I once sat beside Shaul Mofaz in the Knesset chamber, and he told me about those moments after the terror attack in Netanya. Mofaz, who was then chief of staff, had spent Seder night with soldiers at an outpost. He called Prime Minister Sharon, and they decided to break the rules of the game and implement Operation Defensive Shield, to occupy the cities that were under Palestinian rule. That night, the government held an emergency meeting, and formulated the following decision, in terms unprecedented for that period following the Oslo agreements:

The government has called a special meeting tonight following the severe escalation in Palestinian terror. In principle, the government has authorized a broad operational plan to fight Palestinian terror. Israel will act to defeat the Palestinian terror infrastructure in all its components, and for this purpose, it will implement broad activity until this goal is achieved. Arafat, who established a coalition of terror against Israel, is an enemy, and at this stage he will be isolated. The government has authorized calling up the reserves, as deriving from the operational need, to enable the IDF to perform continuous activity for an extended period and at additional terror centers.*

The brigade commanders were the ones who gave the political echelon the confidence to enter on foot into cities in Judea and Samaria. They were led by Golani Brigade Commander Chico Tamir, Paratrooper Brigade Commander Aviv Kochavi, and Gal Hirsch, Chief of Operations of Central Command. These creative and powerful officers led the defense activities for the IDF senior command, each in his own style.

At the Egoz Unit headquarters in the north, we team leaders received our mission from Company Commander Udi. Golani Brigade was charged with occupying Ramallah and taking control over the Mukata'a, the PA government compound where Arafat's office was located.

"When?" I asked Udi.

"Tonight," he answered calmly, and we returned to our maps and aerial photographs.

The plan was for Egoz Unit to lead the brigade when advancing toward the targets and take control of structures at key positions at the city entrance, thus enabling Battalion 51 and other forces to attack and occupy the Mukata'a compound. My team was once again given the task of acting as advance team and navigating the brigade on the path to the target. I was already familiar with the navigation route from the previous incident, which proved crucial

* From the website of the Prime Minister's Office.

in the extreme weather that surprised us that night. During the battle plan briefing, I was disappointed to receive the order that two marksmen from the special central anti-terror unit would be joining my team.

Passover is also called the holiday of spring, but everyone who was on the march to Ramallah on that first night of Operation Defensive Shield remembers it as one of the rainiest, coldest nights of the year, with heavy fog and torrential hail.

"Commander to One. Begin movement. Good luck," I hear Udi's command through my headset, known as a "Madonna" in army slang. I look behind and see an endless line of combatants moving behind me. As a commander, I feel the weight of responsibility combined with enormous power.

Soon we discover that the layers of thermal undershirts, special stormproof suits and even our broad experience in Lebanon were not enough to withstand the cold and rain, which penetrated the nylon suits and soaked our uniforms, causing our body temperatures to plummet even faster. The worst problem was our freezing hands, which we had to use to hold the freezing metal guns and weapons. Despite the heavy fog, the advanced night vision gear attached to my brow enabled me to identify the correct route, so that hundreds of soldiers bearing heavy equipment could move forward without slipping into the riverbed on our right.

Four years later, during the Second Lebanon War, on the way to Bint Jbeil, a number of soldiers carrying heavy burdens slipped down the hill. The choice of the right path, while accounting for the components of speed and the defined length of time, while considering the fighters' abilities and burden of equipment on their backs, represents a complex challenge for every commander when leading a force.

We reach the preparation area in open territory. At the commanders' observation point, we can just barely make out the structures where we are supposed to take control. At this stage, the companies split up as planned, and each one moves off on its own mission.

My company turns right and begins to climb the hill where our targets are located.

"One, this is subordinate. One, this is subordinate. Stop!" Over the radio I hear the team sergeant who is bringing up the rear.

"This is One. What happened?"

"The guys from the special forces collapsed. They say they can't go on. What should I do?" he reports, referring to the two combatants from the special anti-terror unit who had joined us that morning.

I was furious at myself for agreeing to accept them. In the anti-terror unit, which is an outstanding unit, the marksmen are relatively senior fighters who receive this position just before they are released. There is a professional explanation for this: the marksman is supposed to be calm and able to remain in position at his gunsights for extended periods. He must be able to study the target and shoot at the precise time and with extreme accuracy. The assumption is that an older person can carry out this job better than a younger, more energetic member of the unit.

At any rate, in those moments outside of Ramallah, I was completely uninterested in any rational explanation for why the marksmen had decided to collapse just then. I moved quickly towards the back of the line and saw them lying on the ground with the enormous packs of marksmen's weapons on their backs.

"Stern, you take one pack. I'll take the other one," I order, and I hear a ripe curse in the background.

"Ready to continue movement. Sound the count-off," I instruct into the radio.

I worried that in the heavy fog and difficult effort of movement we might forget a soldier who fell asleep at one of the stops.

"All in order," reported Matuf, the radio man. "You may proceed."

The tension level rose steadily. The buildings we were supposed to occupy were about 250 yards ahead. Intelligence reported that armed Fatah operatives were in the area, that they were alert and prepared for the IDF to attack the city. The fog was still heavy, and the company commanders, led by Udi, met at a point in front of the troops to perform another surveillance and try to identify the targets in a more exact manner.

At that moment, something happened that could easily have become a great disaster and even bring the entire operation to a halt. In front of us, about twenty yards away, we saw a large group of armed men moving toward us from the right. We rapidly prepared to open fire.

"Stop! Don't shoot!" Udi ordered over the radio, and made sure that each commander received the order and relayed it to all his soldiers.

"That's C Company," Udi reported, thus preventing friendly fire that might have ended very painfully. In that thick fog, C Company had moved farther south than planned and crossed over the margin of our section. This is something that happens on occasion during battle, and that is likely to happen again to those of us who take on the military profession, whether in regular service or in the reserves.

In 2006, during the Lebanon War, a similar incident unfortunately came to a different end. In the Haddatha region, a tank from Battalion 53 accidentally ran over a position of Battalion 51 soldiers who were hiding in the bushes. The result was disastrous. Two combatants were killed, Yosef Abutbul and Tomer Amar, and two others wounded. We had tried to explain to the tank commanders over the communications network that they were very close to the other soldiers, but a mistake in navigation and pressure from missile and anti-tank fire caused the terrible incident.

Yosef Abutbul had been wounded previously in the leg during the battle in Bint Jbeil, and after the battle he was evacuated to

Ziv Hospital in Zefat. The physicians gave him several days of rest, but Abutbul refused and insisted on returning to battle with his comrades in Golani. On August 12, 2006, two and a half weeks after he was wounded, Yosef was killed alongside his fellow soldier Tomer Amar.

Near the targets in Ramallah I identified my building, and received authorization from Udi to proceed with my mission. Parallel to me on the left, Pomerantz's team advanced toward its target, the building next door. I decided to proceed with my advance team and try to find an alternate entry point, in order to attack from an unanticipated location.

"Two armed men twenty yards ahead," the advance team marksman reported.

"Yes, I see."

"Prepare to fire!" I announced on the radio, and added that I was about to throw a grenade. The two terrorists were patrolling beside the entrance to the building, separated from us by a low stone embankment. Thanks to the dense fog, they didn't identify us. I pull out the grenade from my military vest and try to turn the safety catch. Damn, my frozen fingers refused to make the necessary moves in order to release the catch.

I couldn't believe this was happening to me right then, and I ordered Matuf the communications man to fire a hit.

"Go ahead, man," I urged him.

"I can't move my hand," he replied, gesturing toward his frozen fingers.

"Open fire!" I order.

The rest of the force that had remained behind under the command of the sergeant joined me, and together we advanced toward the entrance. We entered the building and began to check the rooms one by one. We couldn't afford any mistakes because at any moment a terrorist could jump out from around a corner and open fire. Inside the rooms I saw cups of coffee that were still steaming, and cartridges on the floor, signs that the enemy had just recently fled. I continued up the stairs and climbed up to the next floor with the other fighters.

From the buzz on the company communications network I understand that in the building next door, Pomerantz had encountered terrorists and was fighting a battle. Then I could no longer hear him, and I realized he was wounded. Attar Ben Yehuda, his team sergeant, replaced him as commander. He bravely outflanked and attacked the terrorists and took all of them out. After Operation Defensive Shield, Brigade Commander Chico Tamir awarded Attar a citation of merit.

We finished clearing our building and then set up positions on the top floor in order to cover Battalion 51's attack. Underneath the building Red Crescent ambulances arrived to remove the dead and wounded terrorists. Of course, we held our fire, even though later in that operation and in other battles, the terrorists used those ambulances to move in cynical exploitation of the IDF's commitment to upholding international battle conventions.

The marksmen from my unit and the anti-terror unit prepared protected positions on the top floor. This task was made more difficult by the fact that the building was under construction, and it's not easy to take up positions at windows without risking exposure. On the bottom floor, I place a guard team to prevent entry into the building. This team sprinkles pieces of glass and metal sheets in the hallways so that anyone entering will create a noisy warning. We designate the middle floor for organization and rest.

I quickly realized that aside from the task of covering the brigade fighting at the Mukata'a, I had to give the fighters time to decompress and change their wet clothes. Otherwise, we risked being so cold that we wouldn't be able to continue, and we would get stuck in this building. The team members were well-practiced, and they took turns changing into dry clothes, while ensuring that the battle positions were constantly manned. Meanwhile, Udi made contact with the soldiers in the building that Boaz Pomer-antz's team had occupied, and he reported to me that Boaz was dead. But my brain didn't allow me to dwell on this terrible news. We were soldiers with a mission, and we had to keep on fighting.

Boaz, with whom I had shared a room at Egoz headquarters, was an officer with a professional manner who was full of life. He was also sensitive and wise, and always knew how to give sound advice in a simple, humble manner. He grew up in Kiryat Shemona and followed his brother into Egoz Unit. He was buried in Kiryat Shemona, mourned by his parents, brother and sister.

That afternoon, when it seemed like things were beginning to calm down, I closed my eyes and within seconds, I fell asleep, only to be woken a few minutes later.

"Yoni, positive ID for an armed man at the junction," came the warning.

After speaking with the commander on the top floor over the radio, I learned that the identified man was 380 yards (350 m) from the sniper's position. "The armed man is moving confidently, but soon he'll disappear," the marksman reported. I verified that the shooter was within the border of our area and authorized fire even before I could get to the marksman's position.

The countdown came over the radio: "4..3..2..1..fire." One bullet, another one, then silence. The position commander gave the code word that meant we had hit and killed the terrorist.

"Very good," I said encouragingly. "Don't leave the position. More armed men might arrive soon," I instructed them while running up to the top floor.

The terrorists did show up, but they already knew the drill, so they drove up in a Red Cross ambulance to remove their comrade's body. That way we couldn't touch them.

That evening, we prepared to remove Boaz's body. A team of Achzarit heavy armored personnel carriers was attached to our unit's location. From the window, I watched Boaz's soldiers car-

rying his body on a stretcher and loading it into the narrow back
door of the heavy vehicle. For a second, the blanket covering his
face slipped off due to the angle of the stretcher, permitting me a
fleeting second to say goodbye to my roommate.

In the meantime, Battalion 51 completed its mission and took
over a large portion of the office buildings in the Mukata'a. As
became clear from previous missions and this one as well, the
Fatah policemen and Tanzim activists mostly avoided direct
encounters with the IDF. As soon as we threatened battle, they
would retreat.

Night fell, and with it, quiet. Udi and I chatted about my wedding, where he had been a guest, just a few days previously. I shared
with him how strange I felt at the sharp transition of the past thirty-
six hours: from *chatan* enjoying my *sheva berachot* celebrations to
soldier huddled inside a pile of Arab blankets in Ramallah.

We prepare to advance toward the Mukata'a and Arafat's
headquarters. The political echelons were seriously considering
whether to attack the chairman of the Palestinian Authority, which
was fanning the flames of terror. The deputy commander of Battalion 51, Major Yaniv Asor, waited for us under the buildings with
the Achzarit team, to escort us into the PA government compound,
where most of his battalion was already positioned. We were
given the job of passing through the Battalion 51 area and then
taking control over the office of Chairman Arafat himself, who
was isolated in his room with several guards. We stuffed ourselves
into the heavy, noisy vehicles and drove through Ramallah on the
way to our destination.

A trip in the bowels of an armored military vehicle, whether
APC or Achzarit, full of soldiers and equipment, with the metal
exit hatches closed and visibility blocked, is no easy experience.
This was particularly true for Egoz fighters, who had never trained
in heavy vehicles, and were used to the relative freedom of movement on foot or by helicopter for their missions. I had begun my
military service in the Golani infantry, and I had even been an

Achzarit driver. Still, as I rode inside the vehicle through the heart
of Ramallah, I was very disturbed by the sensation of being driven.
I didn't know where I was, and I had no control over what was
going on. From the radio broadcasts I tried to figure out where
we were at each given moment, in case we were fired on and had
to get out and react.

Finally, we reached the Mukata'a. The Battalion 51 commanders and fighters spread through the PA buildings and established
surveillance and sniper positions. They had also experienced a
hard night of combat, but they were determined to accomplish
the mission, and they succeeded. The battalion suffered one
casualty, First Sergeant Roman Shliapstein. I stood next to one
of the positions to hear an explanation of the building complex.
Soon I would get orders for our new mission, and it was time to
learn the territory.

"Hey, what's happenin'? My name's Gadi," said the position
commander from Battalion 51, introducing himself. Gadi was a
tall, broad-shouldered guy with a smile you can't miss. Through
the corner of the window, Gadi pointed out the building where
Arafat was then residing, and described his soldiers' positions. We
shook hands and said goodbye.

A few days later, Gadi Ezra was killed in battle in Jenin, while
attempting to rescue a wounded soldier. He was awarded a citation for this act of bravery. Gadi had been about to complete his
army service, and he left this letter to his girlfriend Galit, whom
he had planned to marry soon afterward:

With God's help

16 Adar 5762
My dear Galit,
If you this note reaches you, then something has happened
to me.
This morning we received notice that the operation planned
yesterday will be implemented today, with God's help.

I told you that the operation was changed and it's not what was supposed to happen – I didn't want to worry you, my dear.

My love, I feel that on the one hand, there's nothing I want more in the world than to be with you, to love you and to build a home and family with you. On the other hand, there's nothing I want more than to go on this mission and hit those bastards with a powerful blow, so that they won't even consider carrying out another terror attack. I want them to realize that every time they do so, we'll hit them where it hurts them the most, and that we're ready to pay the price.

I'm willing to be that price . . .

I love you and I'll always love you. Know that the only thing that's constantly in my mind is you, even in these moments. I'm sure that the moment whatever happened happens to me, you'll be the last thing I'll think of, and I'll leave this world knowing that I was as happy as possible, thanks to you.

Think about the fact that you made me the happiest man alive, and led me to successes that all my life I only dreamed of reaching . . .

I love you always and forever ever, and I'll always be with you.

Gadi

Our next mission was to advance and take control over the office surrounding Arafat's office, to intensify his isolation and the pressure on him. Company Commander Udi gave me a mission: move out and capture the first building. He would move with my team in the center of our force. Under cover of fire from Battalion 51, we crossed the government ministers' parking lot at a run and reach the entrance to the building.

While running, I catch sight of a blood-soaked pair of IDF uniform pants lying on the ground. Instinctively I pick it up and continue moving. The pants had belonged to First Sergeant Roman Shliapstein, who had been killed forty-eight hours earlier.

I thought it might be important to preserve those pants for burial, since they were full of blood, and Jewish law requires burial of as much of the physical remains as possible. We moved up the steps, and met up with another team that took control over the first floor, and took up our positions.

"Further down the hallway there's shooting every once in a while, and we can hear voices of people talking in Arabic," the others informed us.

I went down to the lower floor to check with the sergeant that all the team members had crossed the parking lot and entered the building. Suddenly, I heard the sound of shooting from the top floor. I pull a hand grenade out of my vest and run up the stairs with the advance force to where we had been just five minutes earlier.

"This time I'm going to eliminate them," I manage to think, recalling the previous incident when I hadn't been able to turn the safety catch due to the freezing cold. We prepare to attack, but Udi pushes an elbow into my stomach and stops me from advancing.

"Let's isolate them," he says softly.

Silence falls over the building again. We realize that the shots had been fired by Arafat's armed guards, who had returned to his room after firing several warning rounds to scare us off.

Military service leads to many exceptional situations, including on the battlefield. Still, in hindsight, this situation proved to be particularly unusual. On the top floor, in a quiet corner room next to Arafat's office, we placed three fighters in front of three holes in the wall, in continuous shifts. On the other side, behind the holes in which the marksmen placed their weapons, we could see Arafat's private room, where he had sat just a few minutes earlier. A large chair covered with gold leaf, an opulent wooden table, the aroma of cigar smoke, and warm air from the heating system evoked the luxurious living conditions of the man who caused the deaths of thousands of Israelis over the years.

In the quiet side room, my marksmen were given the responsibility of targeting Arafat, if authorization was given from the political echelons. The Chief of Staff special operations team, Sayeret Matkal, waited in the door, ready to storm the room, and we stood at the apertures in case Arafat managed to flee. For three days we waited for the authorization, but feet were dragging. In the meantime, despite the high tension and the bizarre situation, close ties developed between the brown berets of Egoz and the red berets from the other special ops team.

"Good evening, this is Commander. Over," came the voice of Tamir, Egoz commander, over the network.

"Who knows how to shoot a Lau missile with high accuracy? I'm looking for a volunteer." Quiet over the network. The Lau shoulder-launched missile was one of the weapons found in almost every infantry division of the IDF. They were easy to operate but difficult to aim. In Egoz, we had developed the ability to use a laser marker to launch this missile, which significantly improved its accuracy.

"This is Deputy. I volunteer. Over," said Major Rafi Milo, deputy commander of Egoz. Rafi, who was known for his bravery, had to shoot accurately at the window of Chairman Arafat in order to deter his guards. Inaccuracy could lead to a political result that was completely undesirable. No one wanted to miss this event. In moments, all the commanders and fighters from Egoz crowded around the windows in order to watch the hottest show in Ramallah. Rafi went up to the roof of one of the adjacent buildings, and using the laser marker, he aimed the missile at the wall next to Arafat's office.

"This is Deputy. Prepare to fire."

Boom! A direct hit beside the window as planned caused hasty movement of the figures inside the building, but nothing more. Over the next few days, we remained inside the Mukata'a, waiting for the political authorization that would never arrive.

Yom Ha'atzmaut, Israel Independence Day, came and went. I

received personal permission from the Egoz commander to leave for less than twenty-hour hours to meet my new wife, and to digest the fact that we had just been married. This is always a challenging dilemma in military leadership. As the Mishna says, "But in a war commanded [by the Torah] all go out, even a bridegroom from his room and a bride from her canopy." When the Jewish state or the people are in an extreme situation, everyone is required to participate in war. In short, I had no real excuse. Still, I decided to take the leave that was offered.

Ma'ayan and I spent an abbreviated Yom Ha'atzmaut night in Moshav Horashim in the north. The next morning, the Egoz adjutant, who had heard I was in the area, asked me to carry out a difficult mission.

"Go to your room at Egoz headquarters," he requested, "and get the personal belongings of Pomerantz, the guy who was killed. His family is waiting for them."

Ma'ayan and I went into the room, which had remained unlocked since we had been called up for the operation, and we gathered my roommate's belongings. Years later, Ma'ayan reminded me of that first painful time when I had introduced her to my army life, there in Boaz's room.

The newspaper pages with photos of murdered Israelis from various terror attacks were still hanging next to the bed, and they jolted me back to reality. There was an operation going on, and I had to get back. I said goodbye to Ma'ayan at French Hill junction and rode a military vehicle back to Ramallah, to my team of fighters. Operation Defensive Shield continued.

From Ramallah, we went to Jenin where we joined the Golani Brigade and continued the battle. The IDF was like a lion that had awoken from a long slumber and decided to make war on terror and its perpetrators: "Behold, a people that rises like a lioness and raises itself like a lion" (Numbers 23:24). The operation lasted for about a month. We continued with our operations, in which the brigades were divided into battle regions, aiming to completely obliterate the terror infrastructure. After the position of continuous defense in the 1990s, the state's political leaders and IDF commanders realized that we had to switch to initiative and aggressiveness.

# Chapter 3

## Continued War on Terror – Helicopter Attack on Teluza

In the summer of 2002, Lieutenant Colonel Avi Peled began his position as the new Egoz commander. He entered the job with a challenging initiative – the entire Egoz unit was to carry out a helicopter attack on the Arab village of Teluza. This village, which was associated with Hamas, was located in the northern portion of Samaria on a high, isolated point. The General Security Services had information about several terrorists who were spending nights in Teluza, feeling confident in the topographic conditions. To trap the terrorists, the plan was to surprise them as they slept in their beds. The companies would be flown in silent Yanshuf helicopters, land at a hidden position in the adjacent riverbeds, and invade the village on foot from several directions simultaneously. Company A and the team under my command was given the mission of sneaking into Teluza from the northwest and stopping terrorists whose identities were given to us by the GSS.

In preparation for the mission, an area in northern Israel was chosen to replicate the hills of Samaria. Twenty-four hours before the mission, we performed a unit simulation exercise with the

participation of all Egoz fighters and equipment, in order to repro-
duce all stages of the operation and prepare for any contingency.

On the morning of the operation, Ma'ayan called. "Yoni, I'm
coming to visit," she informed me. We had hardly seen each
other since the wedding. My responsibilities as commander, the
missions, arrests and other activities meant that only on rare occasions was I able to go home. Often just after arriving, I was called
up for a new mission. For reasons of confidentiality, I couldn't
tell Ma'ayan that we were planning to go on a mission that very
night, and that I had no time to breathe, much less meet. But she
insisted, and came anyway. Apparently the powers above took pity
on us, and the GSS asked us to postpone the mission for a day, so
that Ma'ayan and I were able to spend a few more hours together.

Finally the evening of the mission arrived. At the landing strip
in the north, hundreds of commanders and fighters waited beside
their battle equipment, their faces painted with camouflage colors.
Pairs of Yanshuf helicopters arrived one after another, loaded the
soldiers, and took off toward the target. The flight took about
twenty minutes, and then we landed.

"Forward! Get the guys out, fast," I order the sergeant over
the network. I open a map and compass to orient myself in the
landscape.

"Yoni, we have a problem," he replies.

I run to the helicopter and see my team lying in the belly of
the helicopter, packed in tight among the equipment with no
room to move.

"What's going on here?" I ask, while the helicopter pilot
informs me that he has to cut off contact. After a quick check I
discover that the soldiers' legs had gone numb due to the crowded
conditions during the helicopter ride. Weird, but it happens.

In the unforeseen reality of battle, the commander is faced
with unusual situations for which no training course can prepare him. The last thing I expected in the battle scenario for this
mission was to find myself removing soldiers who were in an

invalid-like condition from the helicopter. In the coming missions, and later in my service as a commander, I drew conclusions from this incident, and practicing correct seating arrangement in a helicopter became an inseparable part of general battle procedure.

The team sergeant and I began to pull the soldiers one by one out of the helicopter and into open territory.

"Daisy (call signal for the helicopter), this is One. You're authorized to cut contact," I reported to the helicopter pilot over the radio network, noting a mild mocking expression under his helmet. We waited for several minutes while the soldiers shook out their legs. The trained team of fighters with me was already arranged for movement behind me. Columns of teams and companies peeked through the darkness from the landing points all around, and advanced on foot over the branches of the riverbed that led up to the Hamas village. Despite the tension and responsibility that I felt as a commander, for a moment I was able to appreciate and take special pride in being part of this amazing group of fighters in the IDF.

"Belgium point reached," reported Company Commander Udi over the network.

"Belgium" was our code word for the stage when all forces were waiting at the preparation point. Then at a pre-arranged time, we would launch a surprise attack from this point on the terrorists' homes. I took advantage of this waiting stage to walk among the soldiers and verify that each force was clear about its special mission.

"Cleared to move out on the mission. Good luck!" said Egoz commander Avi over the radio. I identified the alley that I was supposed to enter. It was very hard to navigate in this inhabited area. In our preparations for the mission, we invested a significant amount of time in studying the aerial photographs of the village. Any mistake in navigation could damage the factor of surprise on which the entire mission relied.

I stopped for a moment, opened the photograph again and

together with the navigator, we identify the house. We reached the jump-off point and quickly completed our preparations, just as in the mission simulation and battle procedure.

I reported to the Company Commander: "Complete," and received authorization to storm the house. The moment when a force enters a building where a terrorist is hiding is crucial. As a human being, soldier, and the first one to approach the door, I focus all my senses, strength and abilities within me in order to succeed in the mission. The first arrests carry with them doubts and even mild fear, but the soldier becomes used to the situation over time. We learn to trust the operational abilities of the fighters to arrive in the proper manner and surprise the terrorists inside the building.

We burst into the house. In the living room, an elderly woman was sitting on the couch. One of the soldiers asked her in Arabic to indicate the room of the wanted man, and to give his full name. We had received his identification number and photograph from the GSS coordinator before beginning the mission. I reassured her, and she pointed to the room. This was when we had to exercise extreme caution not to fire at any family member, child or adult. We had just one mission: to arrest the terrorist. The GSS wanted him alive because interrogation usually led to the capture of additional terrorists in the cell, and prevented more terror attacks in Israel.

The advance force and myself dashed into the inner room, where we met "Johnny" (the wanted man). He tried to get up from the bed, in shock. Excellent – we had surprised him before he could flee or reach his weapon. We made positive identification and handcuffed him. The GSS coordinator was already waiting at the door to the house, and he conducted a preliminary interrogation of the terrorist. We searched the house but we didn't find any weapons. We only found some documents, a computer, and a pile of Hamas flyers with photos of their *shahidim* – "martyrs."

Over the company communications network, I heard the other team commanders reporting, "We got Johnny." The operation was a success.

In the review session after the mission, we discovered that almost all the companies in Egoz unit had accomplished their missions and caught the terrorists assigned to them.

When daylight came, we moved through the village alleys, and then we received the order to bring the handcuffed terrorists to a certain junction at the edge of the village. A military safari truck would be waiting for us there with one of the battalion forces, and it would take the terrorists to the interrogation site.

"Good work," I praised the fighters, and then I gave an update over the network: "We're moving south to the exit route. Make sure to provide cover and keep up battle readiness. The mission ends only when we get to headquarter. Over."

We arrived at the termination point where vehicles waited to take us back to Egoz headquarters. We carried out the equipment check and the preliminary mission review. I looked at my watch – in another two and a half hours, the holiday of Shavuot would begin.

In the vehicle on the way south toward Jerusalem, I mopped my face with a wet wipe and removed all signs of camouflage paint. I prayed that I would arrive before the holiday began, and that I wouldn't have to spend it on the side of a road. Five minutes before the holiday, I opened the door of my in-laws' home. Ma'ayan, her family and my brothers-in-law were all dressed in white, ready for candle-lighting. The scene seemed so odd to me – how could I explain to them that just a few hours earlier, I had been in the home of a Hamas terrorist in a far-flung Arab village? I decided to keep the experience to myself, and tried to enter into the holiday atmosphere.

On Shavuot, we celebrate the giving of the Torah. On the sixth of Sivan, the Torah was given at Mount Sinai, before hundreds of thousands of Israelites who had only recently became united into a nation. On this night, according to custom, Jews stay awake all night long to study Torah. But on that Shavuot night in 5762, I spent the holiday deep under the covers.

The rapid transitions between civilian life and life on the battlefield are an inseparable part of the life of a soldier in the people's army – the Israel Defense Forces. As much as the transition is dissonant and strange, this is how it should be. This is the role of the army. With the soldiers on the battlefront, the civilians on the home front are calm.

* * *

Can we beat terror?

In our time, this question has occupied the entire world, particularly the western side of the globe. Islamic terror in all its variants is challenging a wide band of democratic nations. Some of them are tired of the fighting, while others refuse to accept the full significance of the culture wars. In the diplomatic and academic dialogue that addresses the issue of fighting terror, an understanding has developed in which the term "winning" is irrelevant. To put it simply, according to this type of thinking, we cannot beat terror. It simply exists, and we have to deal with it.

The range of uncertainty has increased with the intensification of Arab terror and the spread of fundamentalist Islam in Europe and in the West. The State of Israel is an island of stability in the region. Over the years, the Israeli government, the IDF and the Israeli security forces have proved that we can indeed beat terror.

The Palestinian format of suicide bombing attacks first reared its evil head in October 2000. Between 2002 and 2005, all the accepted definitions agreed that the IDF had defeated this form of terrorism. Israel's decision to switch to continuous attack operations in the territories of the Palestinian Authority proved to be efficient. These operations began during Operation Defensive Shield in 2002. The effect of "trimming the grass" of terror, time after time, as carried out by the IDF and the ISA (Israel Security Agency, or Shabak), led to uprooting the roots of the suicide attacks.

In order to defeat ideological terror of the type that Israel has faced since the day it was established, the Western world must wipe out two components from the enemy's operation. The first component is the motivation to invest in acts of terror, while the second is the feeling of success that accompanies terror operations. The motivation of Islamic terror organizations is derived from extreme religious ideology. A state that attempts to fight religious-based terror must have long-term national resilience that is deeply rooted in ethical foundations and faith in the justice of its path. Any increase or decrease of terror within the bounds of the State of Israel are direct mirror images of our strength as a society. The proof of this is the Al-Aksa intifada that broke out in 2000, when a debate was taking place within Israeli society and the Israeli government over our right to the land. The Camp David accords were a direct expression of the discussions over this issue. In 2006 the Second Lebanon War broke out, while all elements of society, the government and the security forces were busy with the plan for disengagement from Gush Katif and northern Samaria. Operation Cast Lead was implemented after eight years during which the residents of southern Israel suffered from missiles launched at their houses, hitting their children on their way to school or while playing outside on the streets.

Hamas gathered strength in Gaza and rose to power in the Gaza Strip, and this was a direct result of Israel's withdrawal, without relation to the political discussion. The significance of these events is that the side with greater patience is the one that will win at the end of the process. This patience is derived from ethical and ideological strength. There is no way around determined, stubborn rounds of battle, until the terror organization is defeated.

The second component is to prevent the enemy from carrying out terror attacks. This will lead to impairing their feeling of success. Over the years, the IDF's transition to attack operations in the depths of the terror centers, accompanied by precise, up-to-date information, has created a reality in which time after time, Palestinian terror hits a wall – and fails. I do not mean that terror does not succeed at all, but Operation Defensive Shield and the subsequent operations and constant arrests by the security forces have created a situation in which terror is unable to create a significant effect of intimidation against Israeli civilians. This second component is realistic and measurable, and has been proven successful over the years that Israel has combated terror. As we have seen in Israel's history since its establishment, national resilience and operational successes mutually reinforce each other.

But it is not up to the combatants and professional forces to hold the in-depth discussion on wiping out terror. The sense of mission and desire to protect Israeli citizens has led the soldiers to understand that on the playing field against terror, we must win.

\* \* \*

The team of fighters I commanded was about to be discharged. The security situation and continuous battle against terror strengthened my willingness to continue my military service and in the future serve as a company commander. I approached Avi Peled, Egoz commander, to make two special requests. The first was to take unpaid leave for several months. The goal was to study in a yeshiva and be with my wife. My second request was to return after the vacation to become commander of one of the Golani companies. Leaving the unit, even for a short time, was an unusual request. Operation Defensive Shield taught me that I could be a good company commander only if I understood how the larger army worked.

As a graduate of Egoz Unit, I appreciated the incredible contribution made by the special operations units. Still, it was clear to me that in the next war, those who would lead the IDF to victory would be the major forces and the battalions.

## Chapter 4

# *Shooting in Metulla –*
# *A Matter of Backup*

"Move, move! Time's running out. Unload all the trucks at company headquarters now," the company sergeant major (CSM) of Battalion 13 shouts at the soldiers who arrived from the front lines for training in the Golan Heights.

In the IDF, a battalion means power. Even more importantly, it's impressive to see how a battalion can be moved from one place to another. The movement of hundreds of soldiers with battle equipment – Achzarit APCs, ammunition and tents – to Al Furan camp in Ramat Hagolan was a very complex operation. Every combat soldier in the IDF is familiar with this experience. Exercises, operational activity and another exercise – and sometimes war breaks out and interrupts everything.

I completed my unpaid leave at home with our first-born daughter, whom we named Herut, meaning "freedom."

As I had requested, I returned to the army in the role of deputy company commander in the operational company of Battalion 13. Company Commander Eran Epstein, a professional, experienced officer and wonderful person to boot, met me in the company office at the camp in Ramat Hagolan. Through the window in the

53

background, I could see soldiers and commanders setting up tents and unloading equipment from trunks. They were preparing to decorate the company's designated area in the best tradition of Golani Brigade. Next to the CSM's tent, two huge speakers were playing the greatest hits of popular Israeli singer Ofer Levi: "The stars in the heavens are witness to a dream-like love." The song played over and over again, as if the disc was caught inside the CD player.

After a short introduction, Epstein informed me that we were preparing for a major battalion exercise that was planned for the following week in the hills of the northern Jordan valley. The next week we began the exercise. Moving the battalion at night, accompanied by tanks, artillery and lookouts, enabled the progress of hundreds of battalion fighters toward the targets. I was pleased with the decision to switch to service in the battalions, before accepting the position of Egoz Unit company commander, as I learned a great deal of material and internalized the power of the combat battalions. The short exercise on the beautiful Golan Heights ended with a big company barbecue along with a sing-a-long of popular songs.

Then we switched to challenging operational activity in the Jenin sector. Battalion Commander (BC) Nir Solomon gave the company the task of maintaining readiness to carry out arrests in the towns and villages in the sector. In mid-2003, one year after Operation Defensive Shield, the GSS and the IDF were busy preventing terror attacks on Israel's home front and destroying hotbeds of terror in Judea, Samaria and the Gaza Strip.

Almost every night we were busy with an arrest or other mission related to catching terrorists. The daily schedule looked like this: return from an arrest at four a.m.; three or four hours of sleep in uniform, battle-ready; in the daytime, a GSS warning and setting up roadblocks that lasted until the evening. At the same time, we would receive an arrest mission for the night, carry out a hasty battle procedure and prepare for the mission. During the late hours of the night, we advanced on foot or in vehicles, carried out the mission, and then returned to base to begin another round.

As deputy company commander, I was supposed to lead the arrest missions from beginning to end, whenever Epstein was off duty or his schedule meant he couldn't do so himself. With time, we developed a relationship of professional, friendly trust and shared the job of leading the missions.

I recall the first time I was called upon to lead a Golani company in an arrest mission. This was in the village of Kabatia. Until then, I had been leading a small force in the order of battle (ORBAT), a team of a few fighters. Commanding seventy soldiers divided into three divisions would definitely be a different kind of command experience.

"Tonight your company's going out on an arrest in Kabatia," said Elbaz, the deputy battalion commander (DBC). "Be ready for a long march," he added.

That night we progressed on foot from a hill in northern Samaria toward the village, after the ISA had instructed us to arrest three wanted men in the area. When I looked back at the dozens of soldiers behind me, I recognized the weight of responsibility for the mission and for their lives. My brain buzzed as I pictured the possible scenarios and their solutions in my head. "If they shoot from the upper story of that building, I'll leave a platoon as a holding force and outflank. If we hit an explosive device at the junction, which force is closest to us and can come extract us? How do we cross this narrow alley from the left in a secure manner?"

Once, top commando Meir Har Zion was asked how he managed to act correctly and swiftly in every encounter with the enemy, he replied that for every step he took in the field, he imagined how he would react if the enemy suddenly appeared. This advice helped me in several incidents during my service.

The arrest was successful, and all the terrorists were safely escorted to prison.

We had several months of activity in another sector south of Mt. Hebron, and prepared for another short training exercise with the new battalion commander. Epstein also finished his job and moved on. Towards the end of the exercise, which was designed to create balance between the new commanders and the battalion, we were informed that our next operational sector would be in the north, on the Lebanese border.

After extensive activity against twenty-first century terror in Judea and Samaria, moving up to the quiet, pastoral north seemed like a refreshing and auspicious change. But as usual in the army, the reality surprised me more than I had anticipated, and influenced my further path as a commander.

## "DAVID IS DEAD"

The scene was the apple orchards of the northern tourist town of Metulla. The hiking paths of Nahal Ayoun and nearby Canada Park, the flowing waterfalls and the varied plant life created a misleading atmosphere in this explosive region all along the fence marking the border between Israel and Lebanon. The Lebanese villages of Kila, Adaisa and the town of Al Khayyam were located just two and a half miles (4 km) from the fence, a distance which did not permit the commander of this sector to settle back and relax in the pastoral landscape.

Our battalion was given the mission of defense along a section of the northern border. This meant preventing penetration of terrorists and protection of the Israeli settlements in the sector. C Company was ordered to camp at the edge of Metulla and carry out ambushes along the border in the apple orchards. The nights were foggy, and we jumped whenever anything touched the electric fence. We patrolled until we heard the code word for return to normal, when we could go back to base for a few short hours of sleep.

The High Holidays arrived. The company commander and I divided our leave rotations so that I would be with my family on Rosh Hashanah, and the commander would have leave on Yom Kippur while I took over command of the sector in his absence. On Yom Kippur 2003, the State of Israel marked the thirtieth anniversary of the Yom Kippur War, which had resulted in many casualties. The company was deluged with gifts and candy from the children of northern Israel, who took this opportunity to spoil us. Among the gifts, I found a disk of songs from the Yom Kippur War, which I still listen to with my family. Yehoram Gaon's voice burst from the stereo as he sang "I promise you, my little girl, that this will be the last war." As we got organized for the holiest day of the year, I hadn't received any exact intelligence that the Hezbollah were intending to carry out a terror attack. I had an intuition, a feeling I can't explain in words, that something was about to happen on that day, the most special day of the year. Possibly, my knowledge of the Yom Kippur War and the many books I had read on the topic led to my subconscious preparation for an unexpected event.

Some three years after that Yom Kippur, I found myself in the heart of southern Lebanon, listening over the communications network to the voices of my comrades as they fought a complex battle in Bint Jbeil. Then as well, as if out of nowhere, I seemed to hear the recordings of the brave and daring soldiers who fought on the banks of the Suez Canal in 1973. Those voices urged me to take action and not stand on the sidelines.

But before the fast began on that Yom Kippur in 5764–2003, the company commander and myself met to coordinate the company activity, which included an ambush of a point on the fence that the lookouts could not see clearly, and preparing to fortify the patrols and the first response teams.

In the afternoon, after the Mincha prayer service, we began to read the Book of Jonah: "The word of the Lord came to Jonah son of Amitai, saying: 'Arise, go to Nineveh, the great city, and proclaim against it, for their evil has come before Me.'"

"Yoni, report to the war room. Urgent," came the call from the operations sergeant. Then came the repeated order over the PA system: "First response team, real-time call-up." I get an update that shots were fired at an ambush force of ours in the apple orchards west of Metulla, from the direction of Kila. I run to the vehicle along with my advance command post, and we begin to drive toward the incident. The first response team follows behind us, ready with their equipment.

"This is Deputy." I get on the radio to the commander of the ambush force. "I need an exact report. Over."

His quick update tells me that precise shots were fired at our forces and that we have an injured soldier. At this stage, the soldiers are returning fire toward the source of the shooting, at the hilltop opposite them, where the village is located. From my knowledge of the territory and the routes, I know that the trip to the site of the incident would take about seven minutes. I order the war room to inform the battalion forces about the incident and to move the tanks at the neighboring post into shooting positions. My brain was working furiously. I decided to stop and get out of the vehicle with the team a few dozen yards before the incident site, in order to avoid entering territory that the enemy controlled under fire. Simultaneously, the company patrol under Sergeant Isaac advanced from the other direction, firing machine guns into the area. We moved quickly on foot among the apple orchards and advanced to the injured force.

The ambush was made up of the snipers' squad in Gregory's company. The combatants had carried out the regular battle procedure just before the fast, and I had conducted a mission review before the mission began. David, a member of the snipers' squad, had requested to join the ambush team and replace his comrade, who was fasting on Yom Kippur. During the ambush,

David Solomonov, a soldier with initiative and a can-do attitude, identified suspicious movements in the village opposite. He decided to leave the ambush position in the orchard in order to view what was going on through the binoculars, and that's exactly where he was wounded.

When I arrived at the site with the first response team, I saw David lying on his back, head split open by a sniper's bullet. I can't recall the details, the exact timing or the actions I performed at that moment, but the image of David lying there is engraved in my memory.

Shortly afterward, the battalion commander arrived and joined me in the field. I asked him to authorize tank fire at the source of the enemy fire, but the authorization wasn't given. In 2003, just three years after the IDF had withdrawn from Lebanon, the Northern Command had no desire to escalate the situation. Hezbollah gained power under our noses until 2006, then came the Second Lebanon War, and these were part of the price we paid for the IDF's retreat from the security zone in southern Lebanon. The "Four Mothers" citizens' organization, established to pressure the government to withdraw from Lebanon; soldiers wounded and killed in confrontations with terrorists and in roadside charges exploding for eighteen years; and inward-focused public dialogue all led to a situation in which civilians in the northern settlements remained on the front while the soldiers returned home.

Deep inside, I boiled with anger when the battalion and soldiers were prevented from significantly silencing the village that was controlling us topographically.

"Fire!" I ordered over the network. Under cover of fire we laid David's body on a stretcher and pull it onto the road to a point that an ambulance could access easily and securely. According to regulations, only a doctor could determine death in the field. But to us it was clear: our friend David was dead.

Night fell and the sky darkened. In the final light, I positioned

lookout forces over the area and informed the rest of the company forces to report to the post for a discussion. The battalion
commander and I arrive together and update the soldiers about
the incident and David's death. Presenting the details of an incident, as difficult as it may be for the soldiers in the unit in which
it takes place, enables time for questions, updates, to remove the
cloud of uncertainty and expression of the initial feeling of loss.
These details are a significant part of digesting an incident with
wounded. Of course, in war, or in an operation with a series of
battles, this is not always possible, but it can also be carried out
over the communications network.

After the discussion, I go to the office to perform the preliminary mission review, and then return to the field. When this is
done as close as possible to the time of the event, we can draw
conclusions, identify errors, and reinforce strengths. A colonel
wearing the brown beret of Golani arrives at the door of the
office. Erez Zuckerman, the new commander of Golani Brigade,
who had just entered the position a few weeks previously, had
landed at our post. I very much admire senior officers who come
out to the field, especially in moments of crisis. I hadn't met Erez
in person before. He had done most of his service in Shayetet 13
(navy special forces), and had commanded the Egoz Unit when
it was reformed in 1995. Erez had a reputation as a particularly
brave and talented officer and commander.

"Hey deputy commander, is that really the name of your company? Night Predators? What are you, wild beasts?"

Immediately I understood that the new brigade commander
hadn't come to visit for the purpose I had imagined, but mainly in
order to demonstrate power, present a new standard of expecta-
tions as the new commander, and make the unruly Golani troops
toe the line. The problem was that he had chosen a terrible time to
do so. At that moment, the flag hanging on the office wall that bore
the aggressive name of our company was my very least concern.

It was much more important for me to return to the company's soldiers and the forces in the field.

The brigade commander permitted me to interject a few words to describe the recent events. He quickly surmised that our preparation for the mission and its location were no good, and criticized me in short, sharp words. I glanced at the battalion commander, hoping he would react to the challenging situation, but a cold silence reigned in the room. As a young officer, I did not realize that someone had begun a process against me that would prove to have a snowball effect.

David Solomonov's death was very difficult for me. It was the first time that anyone had been killed under my command. Until that point, the soldiers who had been injured beside me were comrades or fellow officers, but not subordinates. Battle is hardly a simple affair, and it involves the possibility of injury or death at any moment, but still, this was a hard moment.

The Solomonovs are a wonderful family. David's mother Evelyn is full of joie de vivre, optimism and love for other people. With a permanent smile on her face and her heavy American accent, Evelyn developed a motherly relationship with me and all of her son's friends, a warm connection that has continued for many long years. His father Mordechai, an impressive man, marched alongside the Golani new recruits for the entire length of the "beret march," the grueling final training exercise, just a few months after his son was killed. With time, my special personal relationship with Evelyn expanded to include my wife and children, especially after we named one of our sons after David. During my service as a member of Knesset, whenever I was interviewed for news programs in the media, I knew to expect a message afterwards from Evelyn: "Nice shirt. You spoke wonderfully," she wrote, even though she didn't always agree with what I had to say.

A few days before the thirteenth memorial ceremony for her

son David in Kfar Saba, Evelyn passed away after a serious illness, leaving me and my family with another painful wound.

After David was killed, tension in the sector intensified and so we had to continue our operational routine. The company soldiers and commanders all persevered in the various tasks we had to perform, granting special attention to the security of the residents of towns next to the border fence.

Just before I completed my position as deputy company commander, I was called in for an interview with the battalion commander. The previous brigade commander, Chico Tamir, had decided that after completing my current position, I would be sent on the company commander's course. But in polite words, the battalion commander explained to me that I wouldn't be sent on the course at that time. In the weeks that had passed since the incident with David, I came to realize that the new brigade commander had put a black mark on my record, and that the company and battalion commanders didn't back me up. I felt very hurt by the fact that in all of the discussions I had with the company and battalion commanders, none of them had bothered to update me about the decision not to send me on the course that I had wanted so dearly. What was more, they had given me a good feeling about my performance in the incident. Above all, I regretted the lack of support. Apparently, they were too afraid to stand up to the new brigade commander, who had a dominant character.

The battalion and company commanders, who were both ethical officers and excellent commanders, advanced to hold other significant positions in the IDF. They proved themselves in battle under fire and were praised for outstanding performance. I am certain that the isolated experience I had with them in late 2003 does not reflect their command style.

When I got the news that I wouldn't be going on the course, I was hurt, and requested three weeks of unpaid leave. I needed time to reflect and make decisions about my next move in a measured, rational way. I very much wanted to command a company, and I believed in my ability to do so. Finally, despite the painful disappointment, and after consulting fully with my wife, I chose to continue to serve in the army that I so loved. My deep feelings of esteem for the IDF and my firm belief that I had much to contribute overcame my bitterness.

Colonel Yossi Adiri, commander of the Samaria Brigade, who knew me from past operations in Nablus, heard about my situation and gave me a call. "Onward!" he said. "Come and take command of an operational company in Haruv Battalion in Nablus. There's plenty of work." I agreed at once.

*    *    *

When I was a trainee in the reserves course for battalion commanders, we spent a lot of time on the issue of backing up the soldiers under our command. This issue was raised most significantly after Operation Protective Edge. During this time, we met with army officers who were interrogated, and are still undergoing interrogation, by the Military Police Investigative Unit and other authorities. Some are even exposed to attacks in the media by various organizations operating outside of Israel.

During one of the discussions, a team commander holding the rank of colonel gave an exact definition of backup: "Backing up soldiers means that you as commander are likely to pay a personal price for doing so. Otherwise it's just a meaningless friendly gesture.

Of course, when backup is requested, the commander must distinguish between a mistake and negligence. A mistake deserves backup, but negligence does not. In my understanding, a mistake means the wrong choice between existing options after exercising individual judgment. Negligence means avoidance of performing the appropriate action. To highlight the difference, I'll give an example from the reality of command on the battlefield. A commander who has chosen to carry out outflanking on the left instead of on the right might make contact with the enemy. Although this decision causes death and injury of soldiers, and although the commander did not carry out his mission properly, his action is considered a mistake. In this case, the commander acted according to the value of persistence in achieving the mission, and did not retreat from that goal. Possibly he swayed in the path that he took to reach the goal, but despite the pain involved, he made a mistake in judgment, no more.

By contrast, if a commander goes into battle without performing a proper equipment check, and his soldiers then lack enough water and ammunition in order to complete the mission, he has acted negligently. This was no case of mistaken judgment. Another example of negligence is a commander who chooses to remain behind while his soldiers attack and endanger themselves. In such cases, the ethic or the right act is completely clear. The commander who was responsible for carrying out the mission failed in his actions. This is inappropriate behavior for a commander in the IDF – an unacceptable norm. Another difference between a mistake and negligence is that mistakes can be used to learn and draw conclusions, but negligence cannot. A mistake is a blunder, no more, no less.

The army, as well as civilian organizations, must aspire to encourage individuals who have both leadership qualities and professional abilities to initiate, create, and develop. In order to achieve these goals, the organizations must give them backup and cover their mistakes. This is assuming that their acts were mistakes and not the result of negligence.

# Chapter 5

## *The Challenge of a Company Commander*

Until I began the company commander's course, I served as special operations officer in the Samaria Brigade under the brigade commander, Colonel Harel Knafo. In the early twenty-first century, the villages of Samaria and the city of Nablus served as a factory for suicide bombers, explosive devices and explosive belts, all aimed to harm central cities in Israel.

The intensive work required by special operations in Samaria proved to be a challenging experience. During this period, I was exposed to the underground activity of the various units deep in Palestinian territory, and I learned to recognize the importance and modesty of the fighters in these units.

"Yair, what are you doing here?" I asked my younger brother at the regional brigade base in Samaria, moments before he went out on a complex mission.

"We're about to begin an operation in Nablus," he replied.

My brother Yair had recently completed his training as a fighter in the elite Duvdevan unit. Because of my position, I was well aware of the details and the danger involved in the upcoming mission. Duvdevan, the IDF unit in which soldiers disguised themselves as Arabs, had been chosen to carry out the task.

"Good luck, Yair," I said, and hugged him, trying to hide my worry. Then I went to sit in front of the screens in the command room, observing the Duvdevan fighters inside the notorious Kasba, the Nablus marketplace, and following Yair's every step. I was going crazy from the thought that I was sitting in an air-conditioned room watching my little brother as he endangered his life in alleys crawling with terrorists. I thought about my mother – what would she feel, if she knew what her two sons were up to in those moments?

Finally we received the report: "Done," and we heard that all of the fighters, Yair included, were on their way out of Nablus.

After completing the company commanders' course, I was sent as planned to Carob Battalion, which was part of the Samaria battalion in the Judea, Samaria and Gaza division. During the years of the Second Intifada and the battle against terror, Carob Battalion was assigned the specialty of fighting inside Nablus and protecting the Jewish settlements located west of the city, including the town of Kedumim. Paratroop brigades usually operated in the area east of the city.

Commanding a veteran operational company in the brigades is a professional and leadership challenge that is difficult to describe in words. I always advise fellow soldiers who have begun their service in the special operations units to spend some time in the brigades in order to test their leadership abilities under the challenging, wearing routine.

One Thursday night, after two days of on-the-job training, I found myself commanding the Kedumim sector and the roads in and out of Nablus, in constant readiness to carry out urgent arrests in the capital of terror. I faced the first challenge of my career as a commander earlier than expected – much earlier.

The next night we sat at Shabbat dinner. The company dining

hall, built of two trailer homes joined together, shook with the powerful voices of the soldiers' robust singing. Using the tables as a percussion set, they pounded forcefully in accompaniment to their singing. The soldiers in this company were given leave every seventeen days, not much for an IDF soldier, and they released their exhaustion and longing for home in rowdy songs that created a boisterous atmosphere.

Meanwhile, I stood outside the dining hall while CSM Tetro updated me on the doings of the company cook: "He prepared twelve different kinds of delicious salads, in best Rifle Company tradition." I approached the door of the dining hall, realizing this is the first time that most of the company soldiers will meet the new company commander from Golani, who just landed in their midst. I stopped for a moment and listened to the words sung by the fighters who I would be commanding in the upcoming months.

Throughout my military service until then, I had thought innocently that I had stopped hearing the curses and rude expressions that were popular in the languages spoken in our region: Hebrew, Arabic, Russian and other various and sundry tongues. But on that first Shabbat evening as an IDF company commander, I realized the extent of my error. The disappointing content of the songs made frequent mention of the officers and commanders' parents, and included a host of bizarre expressions describing the regular path of the combat soldiers. This presented me with a dilemma of command: curses, rude expressions and disparaging comments about officers were definitely in opposition to my military and ethical worldview. Beyond the fact that rude speech and songs presented a moral problem, my military experience had taught me that damage to the soldier-commander relationship caused operational problems, both in times of routine and in battle. The beginning of a new role was a perfect time to clarify my red lines as a commander.

On the other hand, why should I begin my new position with

a clash with the company soldiers and commanders, for which the rude songs served to create a positive atmosphere and offered emotional release from the operational burden? It was clear to me that stopping the vulgarity in Rifle Company would only lead to a rebellion, as the infantry in this battalion referred to acts of resistance. Furthermore, on a personal level, I had no desire to get into a conflict with people.

I had exactly three minutes to decide.

"Shabbat shalom, everyone. My name is Yoni Chetboun, and I'm proud to serve as commander of the Rifle Company in Carob Battalion," I began. The first part went smoothly, then came the hard part: "From this moment on, I ask all fighters and commanders in the company to stop singing any song, tune or melody that contains curses or vulgarity, particularly if these are directed at the company commanders. I warmly recommend that you avoid testing me.... Shabbat shalom."

After a few minutes of shock and silence in the dining room, I performed a solo of the song Shalom Aleichem sung before reciting Kiddush. Soldiers and commanders alike refused to join in the traditional Friday night singing. I had a very uncomfortable feeling that the team commanders and even the platoon commanding officers were sure that the new company commander's purpose was to break and destroy company morale.

Shabbat ended. I was organizing my equipment, about to go out on patrol in the sector in the command post jeep, when the deputy CSM burst into my room, panting from exertion.

"Yoni..." he puffed. "The company old hands are all waiting next to the battalion guard post with their kitbags. They've declared that they're leaving the base and going home," he gasped in alarm.

"How many soldiers are there?" I asked.

"Something like sixteen."

My first day on the job, and already I had brought upon myself a difficult trial as commander. But I was 100% confident that I had

chosen the right path. I was beginning to feel clearly that everything would work out in the end, I only had to have faith. I had to
believe in the soldiers, and at the same time, to demand that they
do their jobs. I constantly reminded myself of that.

"Got it," I replied to the deputy CSM, trying to keep my voice
level.

"Tell them right now that whoever leaves without permission
should clearly realize that the consequences of his actions are
abandoning a post in operational activity, and he should be prepared for trial on the way to prison." I was confident in my words
and in the decisive manner in which I had spoken to the soldiers
in the dining hall: with quiet authority. "I'm going out now in the
jeep to patrol the sector. Keep me informed."

The deputy CSM was surprised by my unexpected reply, and by
the fact that I did not run to the guard post to talk to the soldiers.
During the nighttime patrol, I worked hard to remain calm and
demonstrate a "business as usual" attitude, but although my brain
knew I was right, my stomach was churning. New on the job as
company commander, and already on the first day I faced this
challenge... I called BC Nohi Mendel, who was on leave for the
weekend at home. I updated him about the events, and proposed
that he let me manage the situation as I saw best.

"Yoni," he emphasized, based on his wisdom as a commander,
"don't pull too hard on the rope – it might break."

Throughout my period as company commander under Nohi's
leadership, he kept close watch on the company commanders who
served in his battalion, while granting them freedom of operation
in choosing how to lead their soldiers. Each company commander
had his own unique mode of command.

I looked at the display of my military cellphone –the deputy
CSM was calling.

"Yoni, they've all gone back to company quarters. They want
to speak to you."

I let out my breath. "Excellent. Inform them at 2300 hours in the company commander's office. Now I'll be happy to speak to them."

During my first month with the company, the atmosphere was complex, for myself as well as for the commanders and soldiers. I knew that the norms that I upheld, which included intensive individual equipment checks and strict adherence to military dress regulations, were not easy. But I truly believed that a positive atmosphere would return the moment that we as a company achieved operational successes. I knew then, as I know today, that it is the nature of a human being, especially one who wears the IDF uniform, to want to feel that he is contributing and promoting significant activity in his life, on behalf of society in general – much more than he wants to waste his time singing vulgar, meaningless songs.

In the coming weeks, I invested all my powers in created challenging, professional training exercises, aiming to reach a high operational level. Despite the difficulty, I was able to convince the platoon commanders and company officers that mutual satisfaction would come from hard work and successful operational activity.

We practiced undercover stealth, complex night maneuvers in built-up areas, and firing under various conditions. We created an organized plan for physical fitness training that included carrying heavy loads. At the same time, as company commander I waged a battle against the battalion in order to get assigned to the most complex and sensitive operations and arrests. Almost every week, we went out on two or three arrest missions against terror cells inside Nablus. Until that point, the company had never been given authorization to operate in the alleys of Ein Beit Al-Ma' refugee camp in west Nablus. Now we began to make forays on foot into the city, and to initiate operations that led to catching terrorists.

We invested great effort in our battle procedures. Learning the field, investigating the building and the target for arrest, and using aerial photographs from different angles became an inseparable

part of the commanders' work. Before beginning a complex operation in Nablus, we carried out training sessions and movement
inside Arab villages in the area, to simulate the operations. In
parallel, this also served the general mission we had of defending
the roads in the company's sector.

Not all of our efforts were successful. In one of the operations
in the Kasba of Nablus, while the forces were moving inside
vehicles, an armed terrorist jumped out of one of the alleys right
in front of us. For every combat soldier, this was tantamount to a
gift from heaven – but unfortunately, we weren't able to surround
him and take him out. In the last available seconds, I pulled my
M-16 out of the armored vehicle's gunsight and took a shot at him.
The barrel of my gun released a bullet that grazed the metal beside
it, and a piece of shrapnel flew into my eye and got stuck in my
eyelid. I just managed to catch sight of the terrorist as he grinned
and disappeared down another alley. He was so close... Years
later, when I was interviewed for television programs as a Knesset
member, my publicist commented that I blinked too much. I never
bothered to explain that the blinking was the involuntary result of
a shrapnel wound in an unsuccessful encounter with a terrorist...

In the mornings, after a sleepless night when we performed
a successful arrest, we often were ordered to set up quick check-
points along the roads leading out of Nablus toward the major
cities in Israel. The ISA would give the warning, and within just
a few minutes, we had to set up the roadblocks that often caught
terror cells on their way to carry out deathly attacks. During most
of these long, tiring operations, I stood at the roadblocks along
with the exhausted soldiers and commanders. The work they had
to perform with the Arab residents of Judea and Samaria was very
unpleasant. I knew that I could demand a high operational level
from my soldiers only if they felt that I was beside them at all times,
and that I understood the reality of their situation.

I set another rule for the management personnel in the company: "The combat soldiers in Rifle Company must have the best food in the unit, any time, all the time." Each time we returned from arrest or blockade missions, even if it was at 4:00 a.m., CSM Tetro spoiled us with a royal buffet of tasty treats.

We worked hard – very hard.

One crazy night during that time, as I was driving toward the command post after a patrol among our positions in the sector, I received a phone call from my wife.

"How are you? Are you by any chance next to Kedumim?"

"Yes, dear," I answered her. "Why?"

"I'm here. Can you spare a few minutes?"

We were then living in Jerusalem. I was both surprised and deeply worried by the idea that Ma'ayan had driven by herself to Kedumim at a time when the roads were dangerous. I met her on the side of the road just before the entrance to the settlement, and she told me she was expecting. In the tough reality that I was experiencing, that message was so joyous, so refreshing, familial and distant from the blockades and the grueling activity. During my years of military service, in the regular army and the reserves, Ma'ayan has often surprised me with family visits. Once she even came to the border fence during the Lebanon war.

The atmosphere in the company changed for the better, and I felt that all of us, soldiers as well as commanders, understood the power and importance of a combat infantry unit in the IDF. The singing returned to the tables in the dining hall, without the curses and vulgarity, and I joined in the Rifle Company songs. One Friday evening, we had a visit from the traveling broadcast station for the "Mother's Voice" program on Galei Zahal, the IDF radio station. The company soldiers were asked to demonstrate their singing abilities while sending messages to family or friends at home. Later I learned that the person who had asked the radio station to come to us was none other than BC Nohi, who had followed the company throughout my education process.

\*     \*     \*

The beginning of my role as company commander taught me much about the meaning of leadership. I identified two approaches to the issue. The first approach asserts that the leader must identify and recognize the reality of his public, and adapt himself to it accordingly. This means that the leader or commander who realizes that the situation in the field is far removed from the ethical standard to which he aspires, must tone down his messages and reduce his demands, both from the environment and from his subordinates. In this way, he will maintain a positive and close relationship between the sides. The fear that insistence on standards will create a disconnection between the leader and his environment pushes many to follow this approach.

In my military and public life, I have noted how this approach is respected and even used as an ideological explanation for almost any act or decision. Yet such actions often contradict a clear ethical system. All too often, the fear of making decisions that in the short term might not be accepted by society, and sometimes also by the media, leads many leaders to adopt this approach. In fact, in many cases, the lowering of standards for values expresses a lack of belief in the subordinates or in the public that chose a certain individual to lead that society. The failure to identify the high positive potential found in each and every person leads the leader to abandon important requirements when determining an appropriate level of values.

The second leadership style is based on the opposite assumption. In this style, the commander or leader must be committed to two central issues. The first is a world of values that is ethical, professional, and constant. The second is true confidence and faith in the public or in the soldiers whom he leads, that these people truly have the will and ability to aspire to doing good or even better. True leadership is really a call of "After me!" The big challenge of leadership is to motivate soldiers in the direction of a worthy and true value, without reducing or narrowing it. Of course, this has to be carried out in a gradual process, in a satisfying manner and with understanding of the existing civilian or military reality, while constantly aspiring to attain the defined ethical goal.

Above all, this type of leadership requires the commander to clarify for himself the ethical norms that guide and motivate him in his work. The commander must be honest with himself in order to identify when he makes a mistake and leads his subordinates down an incorrect path.

To put it succinctly, it's difficult to be a commander, and even more so, to be a leader.

# Chapter 6

## *Terrorist on Mt. Ebal*

The city of Nablus is located in a valley between Mt. Gerizim in the south and Mt. Ebal in the north. When the Israelites entered the Land of Israel after forty years of wandering in the desert, Moses' successor Joshua stood on Mt. Ebal and built an altar. Six of the Israelite tribes stood on Mt. Gerizim, where they pronounced blessings, while the six remaining tribes stood on Mt. Ebal and pronounced curses. The remains of Joshua's altar are still visible today on the top of Mt. Ebal.

Both hills are strategic locations in Samaria. Their height permits the IDF to conduct observation of the terrorist enclave of Nablus and over the entire region. In addition, a military base is located on top of Mt. Ebal, next to a tall antenna. At one point, our turn came to protect the base on Mt. Ebal, to guard the approach road and maintain readiness for arrest missions in the city and in the Hamas-controlled village of Atzira A-Shamalia, which is located within the company's sector.

The timing of the transition was terrible. Winter had arrived in full force, and the cold penetrated our bones. The company post at the top of the hill, some 3,080 feet (940 m) high, represented a challenge from both an operational and command point of view.

---

"Hey, what's the deal with this fog?" I asked the company commander I was about to replace, as we climbed the narrow, winding road up the hill.

"Be strong, brother," the other company commander encouraged me with a smile. "Don't move without trackers to check before opening the road each morning," he emphasized. "We've had lots of explosive devices here in the past. Terrorists from Nablus can still come up here to plant explosives or shoot," concluded my comrade, ending the coordination and replacement process.

The activity in the Mt. Ebal sector was full of operational challenges. Eventually, our proximity to Nablus and nearby villages contributed to important successes in the arrests and ambushes we performed.

Kochi (from *kochav*, star) was the nickname that the company fighters gave to the reinforced post that offered observational control over one of the roads leading to Nablus and its northern neighborhoods. The position was manned by company soldiers in accordance with the evaluation of the operational and intelligence situation. As Kochi was located a few miles away from the company post, the squad commander in charge managed the daily operations independently, acting as post commander in practice.

"Commander, this is 2A. They're firing on Kochi. Everything's fine. Over," the Kochi squad commander reported one morning while the company was preparing to open a road leading to the hill. From preliminary questioning of the soldier at the post, I understood that a volley of shots had been fired at the concrete structure, but the source of the shooting was not identified. I realized that the shooter was positioned at the edge of Nablus closest to our post. I decided to play the waiting game.

Early the next few mornings, under cover of the dense fog, the enemy repeatedly fired shots at the post, but still we were not able to identify the source. The new commander of Carob Battalion, Lieutenant Colonel Oren Chen, who had replaced Nohi Mendel, ordered me to plan an operation in the area to make contact with the wily terrorist. I planned to use my experience from Egoz to set up a camouflaged ambush in the rocky, forested area next to the first line of houses in Nablus. I instructed the platoon commanders to prepare for long shifts in the field with changeovers every forty-eight hours. The soldiers were surprised by this order, as they had never carried out such missions in the past, and they feared that their ambush would be discovered too early. But I felt confident that if we practiced intensively we had a good chance of success. I felt that this should be part of the basic abilities of every infantry soldier. I was certain that the platoon commanders would understand the importance of the mission, and we began preparations and battle procedure for the mission.

"That terrorist must die!" I insisted to the soldiers.

For the next two days, we trained in the territory adjoining the post, simulating a camouflaged ambush with snipers. I reported to the battalion commander that the first squad was ready to perform the mission. We designated a mobile company rescue force in case the squad was exposed or discovered. After a final briefing and mission review, the first platoon commander began to advance on foot toward the planned ambush point.

Ninety minutes passed, and we received the report that the squad had reached the ambush point. Another forty-eight hours passed, but nothing happened. The second ambush squad went out to replace the first one, with the goal of maintaining continuity. To avoid exposure, the exchange took place at night, with the soldiers crawling several dozen yards over difficult terrain. Time passed, and we continued to hear distant sounds of shooting from the direction of Nablus, but still we couldn't identify the shooter.

As company commander, I set a routine for myself in which I regularly entered the rooms of the company soldiers to sit and chat with them, to take the company's "pulse" and listen to the current topics of conversation. Unlike other IDF companies in the brigade, these soldiers went home only infrequently, and the operational activity in Nablus sector naturally led to some erosion of morale. The talk in the soldiers' quarters revealed much about the atmosphere in the company, the relationships between soldiers and commanders, and the level of motivation. These informal encounters particularly contributed to the creation of a friendly, close connection between myself and the soldiers, even though I was their commander.

One night I was sitting in a soldier's room, as was my habit. In conversation, the soldiers expressed concern about the ambush operation I had initiated at Kochi.

"You're overworking the company. We don't have enough personnel because of the operation, so guard duty, patrols and kitchen duty falls to a small number of fighters," they asserted, justly. They felt that the operation wasn't leading to the expected results. Then, at just the right time, an operations sergeant from the company operations room showed up in the soldiers' quarters. He reported that the ambush force was trying to contact him, but the communications quality was poor.

I ran to the operations room. I recalled the ambush two years previously in the apple orchard on the Lebanese border, in which David was killed. Any report from an ambush position in the field made me jump, especially when communication was faulty.

"Kochi ambush, this is Commander. What's going on? Over," I asked over the radio. I could hear only disconnected, fuzzy words in reply. I was certain that the ambush force was experiencing an unusual situation. "Damn it, now of all times there's no reception," I muttered.

"This is Commander," I continued. Then I had an idea. "If you're in a confrontation, press the radio handset button twice." Two bursts of static came in reply. I gave the order to send out the rescue squad to the planned point. While I went out to the site in the command post jeep, I ordered Tal, commander of platoon 2, to isolate the area and the territory around him that controlled it.

The natural instinct of every combat soldier, and all the more so for commanders, is to rush to the location of the encounter and join in the fighting. Often, this hasty, instinctive decision merely causes more casualties and wounded, since it means that more soldiers enter the enemy's area of control. In this case, as we had planned and practiced, our forces entered in the correct manner for examining the situation and integrating into the encounter. Despite the tension and pressure, I was proud to see the company working properly.

I was able to get close enough to the site to hear what was going on. Then the squad commander reported that through the darkness, they had identified a terrorist with an M-16 moving toward Kochi, and a sniper had shot him in the head.

"Excellent. Good work," I replied. "Continue with the ambush at the site. More armed terrorists might follow the shooting and arrive at the scene."

I continued on foot toward the ambush location along with a combat squad. One of the company lookouts reported suspicious movements in the mosque next to the encounter location, at the edge of Nablus. I instructed the forces to surround the building and wait for authorization. The commander of the ambush force surveyed the territory to verify that the terrorist holding the gun was dead.

Moving rapidly, the commanders and fighters isolated the mosque within several minutes. After the preliminary tension had dissipated, I was able to enjoy watching them operate professionally, with true motivation and fighting spirit. Next to the body of the terrorist, we found an IDF-issue M-16, apparently stolen. We took the weapon, photographed the body and took his identification documents.

Authorization to break into the mosque was not given. We were instructed by battalion and brigade headquarters to return to our post. I was about to complete my rotation as company commander, and I knew that this was probably my last mission with these soldiers. I grabbed the radio handset and reported excitedly: "Ebal stations, this is Commander. Mission accomplished. Your work was exceptional. We're returning to the post to continue our work. Good job. Over."

One after another, the commanders answered me with particular crispness, using the accepted radio signal: "Roger!"

\* \* \*

Each time I hear the word "Roger" over the communications network, whether in training, operations, or war, a slight shiver runs through me, as this concise word expresses the soldier's willingness to carry out the mission he is given, which is to ensure the security of the citizens of the State of Israel. To me, "Roger" is like the phrase "Here I am" used by Abraham, father of the Jewish people, in answer to the Creator when asked to sacrifice his son Isaac: "God tested Abraham, and He said to Him: 'Abraham!' And he said, 'Here I am.' And He said, 'Please take your son, your only one…'" (Gen. 22:1–2).

Based on this verse, Hannah Senesh wrote:

*A voice called, and I went,*
  *I went, because it called.*

When I became a battalion commander in the reserves, I chose "Willing to serve" as our battalion slogan, inspired by the leaders of the Jewish people in whose steps we walk. Over the many years of Jewish and Israeli history, the phrase "Here I am" has become the symbol of dedication to our values as a nation. It means willingness to perform any mission, to fulfill any need of the state and the people. Throughout my service as a commander in the IDF, in the regular army and the reserves, and in my public service career, I have witnessed thousands of young men and women who choose to act this way, without consciously stating "Here I am." Despite repeated attempts to ascribe Western values of individualism to today's youth, I am confident that the situation in reality is much better.

\* \* \*

We returned to the Mt. Ebal post fully satisfied, as we had defined a goal and reached it – we had prevented a terrorist from continuing his despicable attempts to harm soldiers and civilians. In the company review that I carried out after the encounter, I noticed something unusual. Dima, the sniper who had shot the terrorist, was very quiet and barely participated in the review, although he had been a central figure in it.

"What's going on, Dima?" I asked him later in the dining room. A vague mumble in Russian signaled to me that Dima was deeply disturbed by the incident. I quickly realized that when a sniper aims at a man's head from a relatively short distance through a lens that magnifies at a power of ten, and hits the target, the sight that he sees is not particularly pleasant.

My forceful handshake and words of praise lightened the atmosphere somewhat. In retrospect, as a commander I should have enlisted professional assistance to handle the situation. Taking the life of the enemy in order to defend Israeli citizens is an inseparable part of the military system. In itself, the act of killing is in opposition to Jewish values and character, but these are also the sources of our strength as a nation and society. When we are required to use it, Israeli heroism reveals itself in its most admirable form without confusion or fear, without doubt. The IDF and the State of Israel are founded on the moral, historical and biblical right of the Jewish people to live our lives to the fullest in our small but beautiful country. Should anyone dare act to take Israeli lives, we have the moral obligation to strike rapidly and destroy him.

Along with BC Arik Chen, we wrote a summary document of the incident that noted errors, strong points, and areas for improvement, for presentation to the commander of Samaria Brigade, Colonel Yuval Bazak. Before we showed it to him, I asked to see the printed document. To my shock, I saw that the photo of the dead terrorist in the field was attached to the first page. I considered this unnecessary, as I saw no reason for people to become inured to the sight of corpses and blood. I asked that the first page with the photo be removed, and only then did I enter the brigade review.

Lior Shushan, the previous deputy company commander, returned from the company commanders' course to take over my position. From my acquaintance with him, I was confident that he would push the company forward. Lior had a particularly forceful manner, which was vital for a sector such as Nablus.

I had enjoyed a special and challenging period with the soldiers and commanders in Rifle Company of Carob Battalion. I had learned an important lesson in faith in our path and in other people. We proved to ourselves that with intensive, professional work, we could set high goals and achieve them.

Any company commander in the infantry who lives with his fighters twenty-four hours a day reveals all of his positive and negative characteristics. It's impossible to hide or whitewash a personality. I made errors during my service, and admitted my weaknesses, but I also aspired to constantly learn and correct myself. When I completed my position, Samaria Brigade Commander Yuval Bazak gave me a copy of *Leadership*, a book written by former New York mayor Rudolph Giuliani, with an inscription that warmed my heart after that very challenging period in my life:

> *Yoni,*
>
> *Congratulations on completing your position as Commander of Carob Company.*
>
> *For a fascinating and challenging period of wide-ranging operational activity on behalf of Israel's security,*
>
> *For the modest and confident style in which you commanded your soldiers,*
>
> *Well done.*

I have read Giuliani's book several times.

I enjoyed several weeks' vacation with my family, and especially with my children, who hadn't seen their father for a long time. I wasn't aware of just how much I would need that rest and family time before returning to Golani in the position of operations officer in Battalion 51. A few months later, Battalion 51 found itself on the front of war in Lebanon.

## Chapter 7

# *Back to Golani – Back up North*

Battalion 51 of Golani Brigade is known as force that attracts fire. In many of the operational incidents of Golani Brigade in Israel's wars over the years, this battalion has been caught up in challenging, complex combat with significant loss of life. These have included the battle at Tel Azaziat during the Six Day War; the battle over Mt. Hermon during the Yom Kippur War; the battle of Beaufort and the Jordan Valley during the First Lebanon War; the occupation of the Mukata'a (Arafat's offices) in Ramallah and fierce battles in Nablus during Operation Protective Edge, for which the battalion was granted the Chief of Staff's citation; and the battle of Bint Jbeil and attack operations in the Gaza Strip, which earned the battalion another citation.

Among the IDF units, Battalion 51 is also known for its combat spirit and exceptional atmosphere of unity that has become a tradition. This unity sometimes presents a challenge to its commanders. On occasion, when the soldiers in this battalion have been displeased with a situation, they have rebelled against the commanders.

In mid-2006, under the command of Lieutenant Colonel Yaniv Asor, who later became Golani Brigade commander, the battalion received operational responsibility for the Ramim ridge sector in the Lower Galilee. The battalion headquarters was located in a post next to Moshav Margaliyot, and the companies acted to defend the settlements in the sector along the Lebanon border fence.

I once more donned my brown beret, and arrived at the gate of battalion headquarters.

"Yoni, how ya' doin'?" I was greeted at the entrance by DBC Major Roi Klein, with that special smile and laugh that was only his. I barely managed to answer as Klein began to explain that "there was work to do," and that he would speak to me later.

The transition to a headquarters position in a combat brigade, after years when I had been commanding soldiers, was not easy for me. Writing orders, administrative details, managing the operations room and war room, and routine work alongside the brigade commander – this was a different kind of challenge than what I had been used to, and I very much missed the direct contact with the soldiers. Of course, I was pleased at the opportunity to return to Golani Brigade and work at the heart of operational activity. In the best Golani tradition, Brigade Commander Yaniv Asor was an experienced, forceful commander who demanded these qualities from his subordinates and soldiers. I took advantage of my new position in order to learn from him about the art of command.

Since the IDF left Lebanon in 2000, the Hezbollah openly set up a series of outposts along the border with Israel. From the Israeli settlements along the border fence, we could easily spot Hezbollah flags and their fighters walking around in uniforms and carrying binoculars. This was deceptive, considering the fact that at the same time, Hezbollah was arming itself with tens of thousands of missiles aimed at the Israeli home front and at IDF forces in the region.

The main threats were defined by kidnapping soldiers or civilians, and penetrating Israeli settlements. These issues occupied all levels of command and the military forces in the sector, including Battalion 51. In the year before the Second Lebanon War, there were frequent incidents on the Lebanon border that were actual battles, including exchanges of fire between IDF and the Hezbollah and shooting missiles and high-trajectory weapons inside Israeli territory. All this was happening while we continued to thwart kidnapping attempts.

I had become acquainted with the sector when I was deputy company commander in the area. It was while I was in that position that First Sergeant David Solomonov was killed by a Hezbollah sniper. I was well aware that the region was illusory and the scenery created a feeling of calm, when in fact it was sitting on a barrel of explosives. In 2006, in the months when Battalion 51 operated on Ramim ridge, the alert level for a kidnapping incident was particularly high.

BC Yaniv Asor, A Company Commander Yisrael Friedler, C Company Commander Alon Hachima, and the commander of the assisting company, Natan Jamber, along with all of the soldiers, worked night and day on ambushes and patrols, on constant alert for terrorist penetrations. The weight of responsibility and fear of a strategic incident of kidnapping a soldier or penetration and harm to civilians meant that we all had to maintain a high level of operational tension. Sleep was a rare and precious commodity.

One weekend, when Deputy Commander Klein was in charge of the sector, I sat in his office along with a group of other officers, in a meeting for updates and to plan the next day's activity. The meeting ended at 2:30 a.m., when at 5:15 all forces had to be on morning alert and operating in the sector. We raced to our rooms to catch a few hours of sleep – every minute was precious. When I reached my room, I realized that I had forgotten an important document in Klein's office, something I would need early the next morning. Having no other choice, I rushed back to the office, counting the lost minutes of sleep.

The office was lit. I opened the door, and saw Klein sitting there, bending over an open book of Talmud.

"Man, what are you doing? You have to get some sleep."

"I'm behind with my daily Talmud study. I have to make up what I missed. Good night, Yoni."

In the army, as in his personal life, Roi Klein constantly defined goals, aimed at them, and reached them. He never gave himself discounts. The phrase he constantly repeated – "Hard is good" – appears above his name in study halls of pre-military academies, as the foundation of their educational worldview.

The intense operational activity in the north finally ended. Our battalion was replaced by Battalion 50 of the Nahal Brigade, and we prepared for a brigade training exercise on the Golan Heights. The switchover day was Monday, May 15, which fell on the eve of Lag Ba'Omer 5766. The soldiers and commanders of our battalion were on their way to the training base in the Golan. I took advantage of the switchover time and the short period without soldiers to travel to Mt. Meron to the tomb of Rabbi Shimon Bar Yochai, since Lag Ba'Omer was the anniversary of his death.

Rabbi Shimon Bar Yochai was one of the leaders of the Jewish Revolt against the Romans. After he was condemned to death, he fled along with his son Eleazar, and hid in a cave in Peki'in, where tradition holds that he wrote the Zohar, the basic text of kabbalah or Jewish mysticism.

Each year on Lag Ba'Omer, hundreds of thousands of people visit his tomb in an enormous celebration in tribute to his life and teachings. Around the tomb, dozens of Chassidic sects dance energetically to traditional melodies played by klezmer musicians on clarinets, violins and drums, while huge bonfires turn night into day.

I showed up at the holy site wearing my IDF officer's uniform, while around me were hundreds of Chassidic men dressed in black. I joined in the dancing. In the center of the concentric circles stood an elderly Chassid with shining blue eyes, holding a painted wooden baton in his hand. He waved the baton up and down in precise movements, signaling the rhythm to the dances and maintaining the formation of circles. There was something impressive about his appearance and authority – like a battalion commander standing before his soldiers in formation.

As the dancing continued, the elderly Chassid in the center surprised the dancers by pointing his stick at me. In the blink of an eye, I was pulled into the center of the circles to dance with the man with the shining eyes.

He gave me a penetrating look and said in a heavy Ashkenazi accent, "Thank you, soldiers, and all the best."

"Thanks," I answered sincerely, and made my way back to the car. This strange and unexpected event at the Meron celebrations in 5766, between operational and training activity and war, often reminds me that despite the dozens of shades that comprise Israeli society after two thousand years of exile – we are still one people. It will take time, but in an organic manner, the millions of Jews who live here will find the right way to live together. I am confident that one day, this will happen.

After two rigorous months of training in the firing ranges of the Golan Heights, we carried out a battalion exercise with the other companies and battalion forces. It was an impressive display of power. After it was over, the battalion officers gathered at C Company's area for a group photo. Sweaty but satisfied, we stood hugging each other and smiling, with the Israeli flag and insignia of the battalion and of Rifle Company C. It was our last photo before the war.

A few weeks later, the rows of soldiers in that photo were shrunk by the battle of Bint Jbeil in Lebanon. DBC Roi Klein, Deputy Company Commander Alex Schwartzman, and Platoon Commander Amichai Merhavia were killed in a heroic battle against the Hezbollah. Company Commander Alon Hachima was the most seriously wounded soldier of that battle, and Platoon Commander Shabtai Ma'oz was wounded in the head.

I framed that photo, and I keep it beside me in every military post or office where I work. It helps me to remember and to keep a sense of proportion about life, and mainly to maintain my commitment to the values that my comrades represented in their lives. Looking out together at the camera, Klein and I have our arms around each other's shoulders in a friendly embrace that can only be understood by those who have tasted the experience of military service and the significance of participating in battle.

After our training exercise was completed, the battalion prepared for a week of vacation at the military compound in Ashkelon, and I planned some family time.

## Chapter 8

# *Call-Up to Gaza –*
# *Gilad Shalit is Kidnapped*

"Ma'ayan, I managed to stuff all of our luggage in the trunk. You can bring the kids out. Let's go!" I called to my wife from the street next to our apartment building in Jerusalem. It was leave time, and we had planned a trip to the north and a few days' stay at Kibbutz Lavi. After a particularly stressful period of operational activity and intense training on the Golan Heights, we had awaited this vacation impatiently. We had hoped to be able to travel with our three children – Herut, Shilo, and Emunah, and finally, after much anticipation, the time had arrived. In just a few minutes...

My cellphone rang. I couldn't answer, as I was busy strapping the kids into the back seat. An "unanswered call" message appeared on the screen, from BC Yaniv Asor.

Every IDF infantry soldier knows that the terrorists have a particular talent for planning their attacks based on our leave time. Ever since I had begun my service as a Golani soldier and commander, most of my leaves had been accompanied by delays due to an alert that popped up or some kind of security event. Why did this happen? That was just the way things were. In Golani, we call it *manhus* ("rotten luck").

"What's up, Commander, did you call?"

"Yes! They've kidnapped a soldier in Gaza!" he replied in a serious voice. "The entire battalion has been sent to the south. Our meeting point's in Ashkelon. Go to the southern brigade headquarters for Gaza. I'll meet you there to hand out orders. 'Bye."

That was all. Now I had to explain to Ma'ayan and the kids that the vacation that hadn't yet begun, was now over. She would understand – she had gotten used to such situations ever since our wedding.

Ma'ayan's first encounter with the call-up phenomenon was just one week after we were married in 2002, when I disappeared for twenty-nine days during Operation Defensive Shield. The second time was soon after that. On the first Friday after the preliminary stage of the long operation, the Egoz fighters were given leave for thirty-six hours. I went home to the one-room apartment that Ma'ayan and I were renting in Elkanah, but barely twenty-four hours later, on Shabbat afternoon, my military phone rang. It was Company Commander Udi, who informed me that we were being called up for an operation in Tul-Karem, a town in Samaria under the control of the Palestinian Authority.

Why did this always happen when I was on vacation? As I said, just because.

I gave a kiss and a hug to Ma'ayan and the kids, who remained behind with the packed suitcases and their hopes of going on a family vacation, but also with the clear, powerful message of "It's Daddy's duty to go back to the army."

On my trip south, I tried to collect information and understand more about the kidnapping. This was back in the days before the burgeoning of social media and WhatsApp groups, and the radio and television stations hadn't yet reported the incident. On the way to the battalion meeting point in Ashkelon, I heard from the company commanders that the fighters had received the report and were arriving at the various transport points all over the country.

The sector where the kidnapping had taken place fell under the command of the southern brigade headquarters. The building was full of officers and commanders from regular and reserve units. As happens only in the IDF, every commander of a force or unit arrived on his own to initiate action, receive orders, and take part in battle, should it break out.

"Amazing!" I shared my feeling with a friend from the officer's training course, who found himself there as well.

"Look around, the entire army's here. This time it looks serious."

Our exchange was cut short when BC Asor arrived and we prepared to receive information and updates from the brigade. Early on the morning of June 25, 2006, Gilad Shalit, a tank soldier from Battalion 71 of Brigade 188, was kidnapped in the Kerem Shalom sector. Under cover of mortars fired along the length of the sector, a terrorist cell penetrated the border, crossing under the fence through an underground tunnel. They attacked one of the battalion's tank positions, and two soldiers, First Lieutenant Hanan Barak and Staff Sergeant Pavel Slutzker, were killed by terrorist fire. At first, Shalit was inside the tank, but then he climbed out and was kidnapped. Moving rapidly, the terrorists crossed the border back into Gaza, using explosives to blast open a hole in the fence. The military wing of the Hamas movement took responsibility for the kidnapping, pulling Israel into a five-year whirlwind of public and political debate. On October 18, 2011, Gilad Shalit was released from being held hostage by the Hamas in exchange for 1,000 security prisoners released by Israel.

"We're preparing for a broad operation in Gaza." This information came from the GHQ operations officer for the southern brigade.

"Great," I replied, feeling infused with a wave of energy. "When is the estimate time for beginning the operation?"

"Apparently, tonight."

We studied the brigade maps and the operative plan that had

been prepared in advance for such events. We identified the area in which Golani Brigade would be fighting. Experience had taught us that the exact details – penetration routes and battalion attack area – would become clear later, after everything passed the authorization of the government authorities and the IDF top command.

Asor went to Ashkelon to update the company commanders about the anticipated operation. As operations officer, I remained behind to receive the text of the first order, the intelligence material and the kidnapping incident brief, so that I could give as much information as possible to the battalion commanders.

A strong battalion is characterized by flexibility and preparedness for any mission it receives, even if it must be carried out within a short time and without complete information. Golani Battalion 51 had this strength. The role of the headquarters officers who assist the battalion commander is to extract maximum information about the enemy, about the various plans that exist and about the means available to the battalion in order to fulfill the mission.

"Chetboun, what's up? Come into the kitchen, have something to eat. You look tired." The battalion cook was the first one I met when I arrived in Ashkelon loaded with materials from the brigade's Gaza base. He also had many years of experience in Golani, and in his own special way he had recognized the importance of the event, and chose to take part in the war effort in the way he knew best. A personal treat of hot *shakshuka*, the classic Middle Eastern dish of eggs with tomato sauce, inside a pita.

The facility in Ashkelon, which on an ordinary day was packed with bare-chested soldiers in bathing trunks on their way to the pool or to a show of a guest entertainer, looked very different. The companies of Battalion 51 and soldiers from other forces were busy preparing equipment and unloading trucks packed with weapons. I could feel the special atmosphere that I knew well, that of a base about to go out to war.

In the evening, as usually happens on the night before a big operation was scheduled, we received a message: "The operation is postponed by twenty-four hours."

From my experience on previous missions and from special operations activities in Egoz unit, which required authorization by government leaders and the IDF high command, I knew that postponements were an inseparable part of battle procedure. Yet despite the delays, I also recognized that this time we would enter the Gaza Strip, even though the IDF had withdrawn from there in 2005. The kidnapping of a soldier is no simple matter.

"I don't get why it's postponed. Are they letting them hide him away in Gaza?!" shouted one of the soldiers, cursing as he packed up his personal gear.

As I understood it, this was an expression of the soldier's confidence in his skills and belief in his ability to successfully manage complex situations. By its nature, the army must aspire for constant progress. It must race to carry out missions. By contrast, the government leaders must apply careful consideration when making decisions.

In the days remaining until the operation was authorized, we moved along with all Battalion 51 companies to a camp alongside the northern border of the Gaza Strip. Sleeping in tents near the beach in the oppressive humidity made all of us stink from sweat, even at the very idea of putting on our uniforms.

The companies took advantage of the time to exercise, practice shooting and train in built-up areas using the Achzarit armored personnel carriers. The headquarters officers, along with the brigade commander, were busy mainly with studying the mission, obtaining constant updates from intelligence, and preparing the battalion and company orders.

At headquarters and the battalion commander's command room, of which I was in charge, I learned to appreciate the young professional officers who came to Golani. Boaz Dorot (Buji), the nerdy intelligence officer from Jerusalem, and Yehuda Levi, the Yemenite communications officer from Elyakim, became good friends, despite the difference in our ages.

One night we were preparing for the operation in a classroom at the new recruits' base at Zikim. "Yoni, can I speak to you?" asked Asaf Namer, a soldier from intelligence. With dozens of maps spread out around us, Asaf and I sat down for a personal conversation. "I want to go back to being a combat soldier. In another two months I'll be discharged. It's driving me crazy to think that my pals are going into Gaza to fight, while I sit here in the rear, preparing maps."

Asaf was twenty-seven years old. Born in Israel, he had moved to Australia with his mother when he was ten. His father Zachi lived in Kiryat Ata, and Asaf had returned to Israel at age twenty-five to volunteer for military service in Golani.

"Are you sure that's what you want to do before you're discharged?" I insisted, pressuring him to see how serious he really was.

"Yes," he replied at once. He looked at me with his blue eyes, and I saw the bitterness reflected in them.

"I promise you I'll speak to the battalion commander. Go back to work."

Twenty days later, I found Asaf in an olive grove in Bint Jbeil. He was lying on the ground next to that accursed wall, his blue eyes frozen in a stare, as shots and fire surrounded us. Asaf Namer was killed in combat in the advance force of Rifle Company C in Battalion 51, wearing his bulletproof vest, ammunition belt, and helmet, weapon in hand. Exactly as he had dreamed. In the few minutes during which I carried his body on my back on the way to the nearby building, I recalled our conversation at Zikim base near the Gaza Strip.

\*   \*   \*

On Thursday, July 6, 2006, twenty days after the phone call from the battalion commander who informed me and my comrades about the kidnapping of Gilad Shalit and the end of leave, Golani Brigade received the order to attack the neighborhood of Al-Atatra, along with Armored Battalion 74 and additional forces. In a battle called "Alonei Habashan," which formed part of an overall operation called "Summer Rain," the IDF prepared to strike in a land invasion with air coverage. The goal was to create a security strip in the north end of the Gaza Strip.

I'm sure that the auditorium usually used for shows and ceremonies at the Zikim base for new recruits had never looked like that. A few hours before the attacks, the commanders of OG2 got up and spoke one after another on the stage that usually hosted performances or entertainment evenings for the soldiers. Before dozens of officers and commanders from all branches of the army, and in the presence of Major General Yoav Galant, commander of the Southern Command, Golani Brigade commander Tamir Yadai described the interfaces between the forces. He explained how the units would assist each other in the complex territory of streets and alleys.

Yoav Galant summarized the evening. His appearance was impressive. His self-confident tone and assertion that "We're here to defeat the enemy" inspired many of us to have confidence in the planned operation in Gaza. On the way back to the battalion's zone, a moment before the operation began, my thoughts turned to Gilad, the kidnapped soldier. Was he still alive? If so, what was happening to him in the hands of Hamas terrorists? Would he ever return to his home and family? The goals of the operation, as defined by Galant, addressed the creation of conditions for his return, but we all realized that chances were slim. The overall goals of the operation were to "exact a price" from the terrorist organizations and prove that the IDF was able to maneuver deep in Gaza.

"Barlev stations, this is Screwdriver. Stand ready to receive orders from Commander!"

Close to the border of the Gaza Strip, I got on the radio to the company commanders and the tank and engineering forces that were attached to the battalion, to verify that everyone was ready to launch the attack. "Barlev" was the radio code name for our battalion, while "Screwdriver" referred to the operations officer. Dozens of heavy armored vehicles lined up one behind the other, ready to receive authorization of the operation. The battalion officers and soldiers crowded into Achzarit APCs in order of movement. Tanks from battalion 74 headed the line along with D9 armored bulldozers, which were designed to remove explosives and construct protected zones in the field when needed. BC Asor and the command room personnel, myself included, traveled in a special heavy armor personnel carrier, known as a Nakpadon.

Finally, the long-awaited authorization to begin arrived.

We were all overcome with powerful excitement. It was no everyday event to participate in such an enormous IDF operation, full of challenge and danger, along with a groundbreaking feeling of purpose. Behind us the settlements of southern Israel were suffering deadly Kassam missile attacks on a daily basis. I felt as if the eyes of the Shalit family as well as hundreds of thousands of eyes of other Israeli families were watching us and praying for our success.

The sound of engines intensified, and the armored monster began to move toward the Gaza border fence. Before turning off my cellphone, I managed to send one last message to my wife: "Good night, Ma'ayan my sweetheart. I won't be available. See you soon." For a moment, the thought flew through my head that quite possibly I wouldn't return from this mission. It wasn't fear, but rather a natural feeling for a person aware of the reality that he was about to enter. This may have come from the emotional need to confront this extreme possibility with clearheaded equanimity.

In the early morning light, we moved at the front of the column. I looked out through one of the slits in the heavy metal vehicle in which I was riding. Around me I glimpsed the ruins of white

buildings, neglected lawns, and pieces of metal and broken play-
ground equipment strewn along the roadside. I was filled with a
deep feeling of longing and sadness, as I realized that the tracks
of the armored vehicles were rolling over the ruins of the Alei
Sinai settlement, whose residents were evacuated as part of the
withdrawal plan. I imagined the children who had played here
just recently, the men and women who walked along these paths.
Not even a year had passed since that dream of peace, and here
we were again, on the way to attack inside the Gaza Strip, with
missiles falling from the skies on the residents of the south.

"Enough. Stop it," I berated myself, and recalled that soon we
would begin fighting at the edge of Al-Atatra neighborhood. In
those moments, the Hamas terrorists were certainly not engaged
in historical reflection on the events of summer 2005 that had rent
the fabric of Israeli society. This time, we had to stand united and
win, we had to fulfill our mission together.

"Barlev stations, this is Commander," BC Asor reported.

Under fire from tanks as well as machine guns positioned in
the turrets of the Achzarit APCs, hundreds of battalion fighters
burst out of the heavy vehicles and attack the buildings as planned.
All around us, the enemy fires RPG missiles, which luckily hit the
concrete buildings nearby, causing only minimal damage. Here
we go! The attack began.

I ordered the command room team in the vehicle to exit with
me and move together behind the battalion commander. With
Alon Hachima leading, we advance along with the fighters of
Company C, mount the stairs of the building and quickly take
control of it. Most of the houses around us are empty; the firing
is mostly coming from deep inside the neighborhood. Yisrael
Friedler, commander of Rifle Company A, reports on the communications network that one of his soldiers has been wounded
and is being evacuated to the rear.

The rapid work of the battalion fighters in taking control over the neighborhood buildings, with the assistance and coverage of the tank and engineering corps, led to impressive success. In just two and a half days, until the order was given to withdraw from Gaza, the brigade neutralized dozens of Hamas terrorists. Battalion 51 alone killed twelve. On Saturday afternoon, we returned to the base. Our feeling of satisfaction and fulfilling the mission was clouded by the announcement of the death of Udi Bassel, a fighter from Battalion 13, who was killed by friendly fire during the attack on Gaza.

We prepared for another land operation in the town of Beit Hanoun in the north end of the Strip. From this location, dozens of missiles were launched at Israeli citizens. We knew that the Hamas terrorists had studied our methods of operation and entrance directions and were prepared for us. This forced us to be more creative and careful. One night, and as part of preparation for the upcoming operation, BC Asor asked me to prepare a training exercise for A Company, under my friend Friedler's command.

After the exercise, which included operational exercises on foot and simulations of terrorist encounters, we sat together in our sweaty uniforms, enjoying cups of steaming and particularly delicious coffee that had been lovingly prepared by Buri, the dedicated company commander driver. North of us, just several miles away, the chimney stacks of Ashkelon rose into the air from tens of thousands of houses. Then we heard an explosion coming from the Beit Hanoun region in the south, the exact area where we were about to launch a ground attack.

"Another missile," Friedler and I grunt together, while we continue to enjoy our coffee. With every gust of air from the nearby ocean, the sweat we had worked up after the intense exercise froze our bodies.

"Listen, Yoni – it's crazy, do you get it? We're both here, just twenty-seven years old, and tomorrow, along with dozens of other young commanders and soldiers, we'll be responsible for the safety of hundreds of thousands of individuals and families in Israel."

I glanced over at Buri, who offered me another round of his superb coffee, and then I looked at Friedler, who had performed an excellent exercise with his company – and I realized that we had no choice. We simply had to win. Over that cup of coffee, just moments before another operation in Beit Hanoun in Gaza, Friedler and I never imagined that just a few days later, we would find ourselves in the window of a house in the Lebanese village of Bint Jbeil, surrounded by shooting, at the beginning of war in the north. Friedler as company commander and I as operations officer would attempt to observe from the window. Friedler would take a bullet in the hand, but continue to command the company and refuse to be evacuated until the fighting ended.

I was soon proven right. Commanders in the IDF often bear responsibility for carrying out missions of national importance. Thanks to commanders and officers like Friedler and his comrades, who place the good of the nation and the public above themselves, we have every reason to be optimistic.

## Chapter 9

# Lebanon – Is This War?

For many Israelis, the morning of July 12, 2006, 16 Tammuz 5766, was just another ordinary day. In the south, the "war routine," a bizarre term in and of itself, did not influence the millions of Israelis who lived outside the range of the missiles launched from Gaza. The Hamas and terrorist organizations had not yet developed the firing ability and the high-trajectory shooting at the central cities, as would happen in Operation Protective Edge. There was something strange about the disconnect between the southern cities, which were missile targets, and the rest of Israel, which continued its daily routine.

That morning changed this situation. As can only happen in a people's army, that morning rumors began to fly around the battalion.

"They're saying that two soldiers were kidnapped on the Lebanese border. Maybe more."

"A tank was totally blown apart by a bomb – the explosion was so powerful that they're having trouble finding the soldiers' bodies."

During our daily commanders' meeting in preparation for the operation in northern Gaza, the battalion commander updated us about events in the north: "Hezbollah has joined the party."

A patrol force from a reserves battalion in Brigade 5 had been patrolling the Lebanese border in two Hummer vehicles, moving from Zarit toward Shetula, when they were caught in a Hezbollah ambush. Three soldiers were killed by missile and machine gun fire – Eyal Benin, Shani Turgeman and Wassim Nazal. Two other soldiers were found wounded in the bushes, and two soldiers were missing.

Under cover of simultaneous artillery and anti-tank fire, shot by Hezbollah along a wide strip on the Israel-Lebanon border, the terrorist force cut the border fence, approached one of the damaged vehicles, and kidnapped two soldiers, Ehud Goldwasser and Eldad Regev, who at that point were apparently severely wounded.

Following the kidnapping, a tank force crossed the border to take control over a strategic point in the area (Flag Hillock). The tank crossed a camouflaged pit filled with explosives, causing the death of four additional soldiers. Then another soldier from Nahal Brigade was killed by Hezbollah mortar fire.

The IDF responded with a massive air attack on civilian infrastructure in Lebanon in order to obstruct the kidnapping and exact a price from the state that harbored the Hezbollah terrorists and enabled them to launch their operations. Division 91 under the command of Brigadier General Gal Hirsch, in whose sector the kidnapping had taken place, requested to call up the reserves and begin a land operation. But at this stage, the government leadership and the top military command decided to continue to invest in the airborne attack. Only small special forces crossed the fence into the areas controlling the border fence and the surrounding settlements.

After the formal reports were received, the battalion officers began a debate over the possibility of bringing Golani Brigade back up north to fight in its natural location. The possibility that a real war would develop in the north did not seem reasonable to us. After a decade of operations in Judea, Samaria and Gaza, our conceptual world mainly revolved around focused, specific ops. We could hardly imagine a scenario in which the entire IDF, including its reserve units, would be sunk in all-out war for thirty-three days, with missiles falling on residents of northern Israel.

Back in Gaza, the battalion commander announced: "We're continuing the battle procedure for Operation Beit Hanoun." The next day was the fast of the Seventeenth of Tammuz, the day on which the Romans broke through the walls surrounding Jerusalem and began the siege that ended with the destruction of the city on the Ninth of Av.

The three-week period between 17 Tammuz and 9 Av, traditionally known as Bein Hametzarim or "between the straits," is known as a difficult period in Jewish history. The Sages determined that during these days of destruction, we follow some of the traditional mourning practices, such as not listening to music and avoiding shaving and haircuts. The book of Lamentations (Eichah) says of this period, "Judah went into exile due to affliction and great servitude; she settled among the nations, she found no rest; all her pursuers overtook her between the straits" (1:3). The Sages recommended taking extra precautions in this time to guard human life. But there we were – about to embark on a *milhemet mitzvah*, an obligatory war of self-defense.

In fact, the historical period between 17 Tammuz and the destruction of the Temple on 9 Av was the last time in almost two thousand years we lost our national and spiritual independence as a nation. The modern State of Israel represents the fulfillment of the dream of Israel's prophets and the Zionist vision – it is a miraculous event of historical proportions. Even in the compelling debate between right and left in Israeli society, the vast majority agrees that the return to Zion and the establishment of the State of Israel are foundational events that reflect the yearning of millions of Jews of all varieties and throughout history.

On the fast day of 17 Tammuz, I drove for a few hours to

Netanya to attend the *brit milah* (circumcision ceremony) of the son of my sister Hagit, who had been born a week earlier.

"Yoni, is this war?" "How do you think it will end?" "Will the IDF go into Lebanon?" When you're wearing a uniform, you unintentionally become a representative of the IDF to the civilians, even if you're just a lowly captain. I wanted to explain to the guests that what was really bothering me was the possibility that they might cancel the operation in Beit Hanoun. The truth was that I had just as many questions as they did. I preferred to reply by keeping silent and wearing a confident smile, as if I knew that everything would soon be better.

"And may his name among Israel be called... Yogev."

I took advantage of the short time before I had to return to the army to enjoy a warm hug from my wife and kids. My father placed his hand on my head and gave me his blessing, as he always did before I left home. As he recited the blessing, I noticed tears in his eyes, and in my mother's as well. They both knew there was no other way.

My father was born and grew up in Paris. As a youth, he had dreamed of making aliya to Eretz Israel. When on vacation from his studies, he did agricultural work on Kibbutz Sdeh Eliyahu in the Jordan Valley. After completing high school in France, he studied medicine in Paris, and completed specialty training in cardiology in Israel.

My mother was born in Casablanca. She and her seven siblings grew up in a Zionist home filled with faith and love for Eretz Israel. On her own, she traveled to Belgium, where she studied to become an optician. Then she went to Paris, where she met my father and they got married. They shared the goal of making aliya after the wedding, and they fulfilled it together.

Today, looking back, when I have my own family, I can say for certain that I absorbed the foundation of my Zionist values at home. Despite the challenges of immigration and absorption, my parents worked to imbue me from childhood with the values of love for my country and my people.

Back in Gaza on the night of July 16, 2006, despite the complex situation in the north, Golani Brigade was ordered as planned to attack Beit Hanoun.

"Barlev, this is Commander Bungalow."

While moving toward the target, Captain Gal Karabaky, commander of the battalion's training company, came on the radio. "My deputy 3 flipped over on his heavy side, he has three flowers," Gal said, reporting that the Achzarit of one of his sergeants had flipped over, with three wounded as a result. The battalion commander faced the classic dilemma of every combat commander: should he use those precious moments before attack to evacuate the wounded, or continue advancing to perform the mission?

During Operation Protective Edge in 2014, my comrade Lieutenant Colonel Erez Alkabetz, commander of battalion 13, faced a much more complex dilemma than this. During the vehicle movement and battalion attack on Saja'iya neighborhood in Gaza, the enemy attacked an APC that had remained behind due to a technical malfunction, and the APC went up in flames. Seven fighters were killed, including Oron Shaul, who is defined as of this writing as a fallen IDF soldier whose place of burial is unknown. Erez understood the complexity of the situation and decided not to stop the attack. The main task was to strike Hamas and destroy the tunnel infrastructure. Still, he decided to designate a force for evacuation and treatment of the wounded.

During the Beit Hanoun attack, after we received the report that wounded were stabilized, the deputy commander of Armored Battalion 74 was ordered to evacuate them. Our battalion continued its mission as part of the brigade attack on Beit Hanoun, and the three wounded were evacuated to Israeli territory for rapid medical treatment. As in the past, in this operation the brigade and battalion forces worked in cooperation with the armored and air forces to kill and wound dozens of terrorists. After some sixty hours of battle, we were ordered to return to the assembly area.

After Operation Protective Edge, we had become used to the routine of short battle procedures and land attacks lasting several days in enemy territory in Judea and Samaria or Gaza. Despite the security situation in the north, the word "war" was not part of our terminology.

After the Beit Hanoun operation, several companies, including my own, were given home leave for at least twenty-four hours. The exhaustion of the last few weeks since we were sent down south overcame me, and I sank into a deep sleep.

"Yoni, wake up. BC Asor's on the phone." Ma'ayan's voice awoke me in the middle of the night. Before I answered, we exchanged glances, realizing that once again, this short leave was about to end.

"We're going up north. Meet tomorrow at 8:00 at Shraga Camp along with the rest of the company commanders. Klein will bring the battalion to us later. Good night, bro," he ended.

"Forget it, they'll just activate the special forces again. They'll leave us battalions behind," said my friend Natan Jamber, commander of the assisting company. I agreed. Our feeling on the morning of July 19, 2006, was that this would not be a war. But the quiet at Shraga Camp near Nahariya deceived us.

"Yoni, what's up?" asked Eyal Assraf, Golani operations branch officer. We were talking over the encrypted Mountain Rose mobile communications device, used for classified updates.

"All's well. Any updates?" I ask.

"Yes, be prepared to attack Taibe. Update your battalion commander and send the battalion intelligence officer to sign off on the area maps."

Taibe is a village just several miles west of Metulla, inside Lebanese territory. We leaned over the maps and studied the area and the foot routes we could use to attack the village. In the meantime, DBC Klein led the battalion's soldiers as they left the base in the south, and traveled by bus and truck convoy to arrive that night at Elyakim Base up north.

We learned that Division 91 operated some of its paratrooper forces together with the Magellan and Egoz special units to gain control over the Maroun a-Ras area and the Shaked mountain range dominating the broad valley across from Avivim settlement. These were both key areas. We increasingly felt that we were standing on the brink of war.

The battalion and companies took advantage of this time in order to train. The firing ranges near Elyakim are very similar to the mountains of Lebanon and, after the recent weeks of fighting in Gaza, offered us the opportunity to regain battle readiness for the Lebanese landscape. I stood atop one of the forested hilltops in the training area at Elyakim, watching one of the companies during a training exercise. The northern landscape was beautiful. After a long period of service in Egoz and Golani, the return to the brigade's natural landscape in the north gave me a good feeling.

"I wonder if we really will go into Lebanon," I thought. As I stood there admiring the landscape, Intelligence Officer Boaz said to me, "Yoni, Benji's dead. An Egoz unit that was patrolling in the nature reserve near Maroun a-Ras took a direct hit from missiles. Five fighters were killed, and Benji was one of them."

Major Benji Hillman was a fellow team member from Egoz. He was a natural leader, a commander in body and soul, with a magnetic sense of humor that drew in everyone around him. After holding several successful positions in Egoz, Benji became commander of Rifle Company C in Battalion 51, then returned to Egoz to command an operations unit. In Golani, Benji was clearly on the path to becoming battalion commander, but he was killed just three weeks after his marriage to his long-time girlfriend Ayala.

To honor his memory, his parents established HaBayit Shel Benji, "Benji's Home," a house and support center for lone soldiers. These are young adults who come to Israel on their own, without their families, and volunteer for service in the IDF, or native Israelis who come from broken or disadvantaged families. The center is in Ra'anana where Benji grew up.

"Has anyone let Shimon know?" I asked. Benji's brother Shimon was a deputy company commander in the battalion. In his modest manner, eventually Shimon also became a company commander in Battalion 51.

During my visits to the families of fallen IDF soldiers over the years, I have become aware of a certain complex, sensitive reality. We commanders and people in the surrounding society who are in contact with the families on official memorial days, anniversaries of deaths, and on the eves of Shabbat and holidays, naturally dedicate most of our attention to the parents of the fallen soldier. The bereaved brothers and sisters are often relegated to the sidelines, and receive limited attention from us. Every once in a while, I try to remind myself of this, but I still haven't been able to carry it out properly, as I aspire to do.

We didn't have time to digest the loss of Benji. All of us, the battalion headquarters, the battalion commander and the company commanders, were busy preparing for the attack on Taibe, under the leadership of Brigadier General Guy Zur, commander of Division 162.

While feverishly studying the operation and the battle procedure, we learned that the operation had been changed. As part of the Northern Command's broader effort, it was decided that we would attack the village of Rab El Thalathine. Frequent changes in the missions assigned to us quickly became an integral part of the character of the Lebanon war. A lack of clear goals and targets for the war on the part of the government leadership and the IDF high command meant that forces were sent in and out in a disorganized, incomprehensible manner, throughout all stages of the war. There was no logical continuity, and this harmed the ability of the battalions and brigades to maximize tactical achievements in the field.

In fact, the most senior level of the IDF avoided stating that this was a war in the full sense of the term. When this concept finally penetrated their consciousness, it was already very late, perhaps too late. In 2005, the leaders of the IDF and the state were busy implementing the plan for withdrawal from the Gaza Strip. This was no routine task for the army. As a result, they found themselves, along with the entire nation, involved on a front that began in the south and moved up north in a series of operations that turned into a war. The lack of courageous leadership was felt deeply, both from a military and political point of view. Israel lacked leadership that had the ability and strength to define a clear purpose for the military process that was eventually called "the Second Lebanon War."

I must note the fact that the atmosphere in Golani Brigade and among the fighters in the battalion was disconnected from the confusion that reigned at the higher levels. We took each assignment seriously. The proof was in the results: in each direct encounter with Hezbollah, the enemy was defeated, despite the heavy price we paid. When we examine the events from a broader perspective, we find that this is true for most of the combat battalions and brigades in all the other units of the IDF, which also acted with high motivation and willingness to carry out every mission.

On Shabbat eve, the battalion was ordered to move to Regavim camp, location of the Golani training base for new recruits.

"Tell me, Chetboun, is it okay that we're doing all these activities on Shabbat?" one of the NCOs asked me.

"In case you didn't get it, we're at war, bro'. Get going!" I replied.

This was the first time that I had defined the reality I was experiencing as war. This time, as throughout my military service, I relied on the IDF rabbinate, which understands the range of operational considerations present in both routine and emergency situations, and their ramifications for the combat soldiers.

On Shabbat morning, the battalion commander and I went to the brigade base at Shraga Camp, where we met with the brigade commander to authorize plans. I managed to spare an hour to join the soldiers in the Shacharit (morning) service at the base synagogue. The Torah scroll was taken out of the ark to read the weekly portion of Mattot-Mase'i, which concludes the book of Numbers.

One of the soldiers recited Birkat Ha-Gomel, the blessing for one who has survived a life-threatening situation: "Blessed are You, Lord our God, King of the Universe, Who bestows kindness upon the culpable, for He has bestowed goodness to me." The congregation gave the traditional response: "Amen. May He who has bestowed goodness upon you always bestow every goodness upon you." I looked at the soldier who had recited the blessing – his eyes were dull and exhausted. His powerful build and the special attachments on his rifle led me to conclude for certain that he was from Egoz. He had been there with Benji, he had fought beside his comrades who had been killed just two days previously. I didn't know him, but still I hugged him tight, while my own eyes filled with tears of pain and pride. I did my best to hide them under my *tallit*, and thought of Benji.

The congregants returned the Torah scroll to the ark. The next time it was opened, they would read from the book of Deuteronomy, which speaks of the Israelites' spiritual and material preparations for entering the Land of Israel. The spiritual preparations were upholding the Torah and awareness of their heritage, while the material preparations were military readiness for war against Og, king of the Bashan and Sihon, king of the Emorites. The Torah describes the direct connection between the spiritual state of the people and their willingness to fight.

## Chapter 10

# Bint Jbeil – This Time, We're Going In

I returned to brigade headquarters.

"Bint Jbeil," the brigade intelligence officer informed me at the entrance to the brigade commander's office. "That's our mission!"

Brigade Commander Tamir Yadai informed BC Yaniv Asor and myself as operations officer that Golani Brigade was being transferred from Division 162 to Division 91 under the command of Brigadier General Gal Hirsch. We were ordered to enter Bint Jbeil along with a paratrooper brigade – again a change of mission. I didn't know why, but for some reason this time I felt that it was about to happen. I glanced at the mission name that appeared on the top of the order: "Webs of Steel."

Back in May 26, 2000, one day after the IDF retreated from Lebanon, Hezbollah Chairman Sheikh Sayed Hassan Nasrallah stood in front of the international media in Bint Jbeil and gave a speech celebrating his victory over the Zionist enemy. The Shi'ite leader compared Israeli society to "spider webs," thus clarifying to the Arab world that Israel's power was nothing but an illusion. Just as a carefully woven spider web is easily torn by the brush of a hand, he implied, so the Arab terrorists could easily defeat Israel and intimidate it into retreat.

I must admit quite honestly that in his speech, Nasrallah touched a sensitive nerve in Israeli society. The decade of the 1990s in Israel, which ended with the withdrawal of Israel from Lebanon in May 2000, represented a watershed in the short history of the state. In the early 1990s, Israeli society entered a painful debate over the Jewish people's rights to the biblical Land of Israel. Major events threatened to divide the Jews: recognition of the Palestinian Liberation Organization as a legitimate partner for negotiations, willingness to give up sections of our homeland in return for peace, the Oslo agreements, and the murder of Prime Minister Yitzhak Rabin. At the end of the decade, a wave of murderous terror attacks bloodied Israeli streets, and the IDF retreat from Lebanon meant that Nasrallah's "spider web" speech poured salt on open wounds.

The transformation that Israel made in the decision to defeat terror in Operation Defensive Shield, and the national strength that Israel's citizens have demonstrated ever since, have pulled apart the Hezbollah's "spider web" theory, time and time again. But that strength is not guaranteed. Israel's investment in moral and educational resources is a crucial component to ensure our continued existence here as a nation. We have experienced low points and crises, such as the withdrawal from the Gaza Strip and the functioning of senior leadership during the Lebanon War. Still, the Israeli public in all its variety has repeatedly served as living evidence that the soul beating within the people pushes the Jewish-Zionist dream to ever higher and positive achievements.

The name of the attack operation on Bint Jbeil, "Webs of Steel," served as a response to Nasrallah's "spider webs" speech given there six years previously. Division Commander Gal Hirsch's plan was to attack the terrorist enclave using a pincer movement. Golani forces would surround and hold the eastern part of the town, while the paratroopers would control the western side. Meanwhile, Armored Brigade 7 would take up a solid position on Maroun a-Ras ridge in the south and fire continuously.

What was the goal of the mission as defined by the IDF senior command? In his book *Defensive Shield*, Brigadier General Gal Hirsch describes the reality that preceded the attack and the lack of a clearly defined purpose: "Then the order came from head-quarters: 'Don't conquer, only take control.' As we were updating the plans, we received another order: 'Don't take control, only encircle.'" Then yet another order came, and in the morning, the mission was defined as a raid, "aimed at severely damaging the enemy and its infrastructure in the Bint Jbeil region."*

The Golani Brigade and our battalion were not at all disturbed by the chaos above our heads. To us, the orders were clear: "Golani Brigade will attack the eastern part of Bint Jbeil and destroy ter-rorists, missile launchers, infrastructure and weapons...."**

The beginning of our movement and attack was planned for between Saturday and Sunday, July 23, 2006. The battle procedure was rushed; we were given less than twenty-four hours to study the mission, give orders to the commanders, prepare the required equipment and move the forces over the border. Still, we felt confident in the operational ability of the companies and combat soldiers in the battalion. Since moving up north, we had used our time for training exercises and preparing equipment and food. The frequent changes of mission and uncertainty were absorbed at battalion headquarters, enabling stability at the lower levels.

We divided the battalion's sector into three regions, one for each of the battalion's three operational companies (Rifle A, C, and the assisting company). Training Company B was attached

---

* p. 278.
** From Golani Brigade's orders for the operation.

to Battalion 52 of the armored division, which also fought as part of Golani Brigade's forces.

On Saturday night, officers and company commanders met at Regavim for the first Operational Group briefing. In those moments before going out to battle, the powerful smell of sweat that rose from the commanders gathered together in the room represented the scent of great confidence felt within the battalion.

BC Asor began by defining the operational goals and the battalion's mission. Then he outlined the details: "Movement begins tomorrow at 8:00 p.m. from the settlement next to the border fence. We'll move behind Egoz Unit, which will lead the movement. Behind us will be the brigade's patrol battalion. Friedler (Company A Commander), you'll lead the battalion order of movement. Jamber (Assisting Company Commander) will follow him, and Hachima (Company C Commander) will close off the movement along with DBC Klein."

Battalion Communications Officer Yehuda elbowed me in the ribs and whispered, reflecting the atmosphere in the room, "This time it's serious. They won't cancel. Tomorrow we're going into Lebanon for sure."

After several days of changes and cancellations, we all realized that war had begun and we were about to take part. Most of the officers, company commanders and soldiers in the battalion had never been in Lebanon before. Since the IDF retreat in 2000, most of the operational service of the combat units had been in Judea and Samaria and the Gaza Strip, fighting against the Palestinian terror organizations.

On Sunday morning I drove with the battalion commander and company commanders to Shraga Base, to the second Operational Group briefing. In the meantime, the company commanders completed briefing their forces and worked on preparing equipment and kitbags for a forty-eight hour stay in the field. The average weight that the soldiers would carry was between forty and sixty percent of their body weight. Everything was rushed, we had no time to waste.

The OG briefing ended around 1:00 p.m. Division Commander Hirsch had arrived to observe the progress of preparations. He summarized the mission and said explicitly that this was a "war." This was the first time that I had heard from a senior commander that the State of Israel was at war. In seven hours, we had to be ready to cross the border fence next to Moshav Avivim.

The platoon commanders and battalion officers received orders to leave Regavim base and go to Moshav Avivim for the last briefing and OG2 at the battalion level, set for 5:00 p.m. in the moshav bomb shelter. It was time to organize my own personal equipment. I opened my vest and verified that all the cartridges were full and that I had enough water for the required walking and the extensive stay in the field. As operations officer, it was my job to form the overall picture of the battalion status at all times and to coordinate among the combat forces and the auxiliary forces that assisted the battalion. The map kit and colored markers (red for enemy, blue for our forces, black for the sector borders) became an inseparable part of my body. As operations officer, these were part of my war materiel. I felt very strange, as this was the first time in my entire military career that I was going on an operation as assistant to the battalion commander and without dozens of soldiers behind me. At that moment, I could hardly imagine that this reality would make an about face, and I would quickly find myself leading soldiers into the horror in the heart of the olive groves of Bint Jbeil.

The path from Shraga Camp near Nahariya to the staging area at a moshav illustrated the reality experienced by the residents of northern Israel, and particularly the fact that the IDF was about to go to war. The roads were completely empty. Not a soul moved in the city of Nahariya, where I was born shortly after my parents made aliya from France. The only vehicles on the road were tank carriers and APCs carrying ammunition and equipment toward the Lebanese border. The signs on the side of the road directing tourists to bed-and-breakfasts in the nearby moshavim reminded me that in normal times, the north in summer was overflowing with tourists and vacationers. I realized that I was feeling and seeing the meaning of the words "home front at war."

*   *   *

When I view Israel in 2006 through a social lens, I realize in pain and sorrow that the Second Lebanon War intensified the tension between the home front and the battlefront. A deep chasm separated the reality we faced under fire from the situation as explained to the Israeli public by the media. Every time we left the battlefield for leave in Israel, we were forced to face this painful gap.

I felt this powerful disconnection after we returned to Israel after the grueling battle at Bint Jbeil. IDF buses transported us to Date Palm Beach in Acre for rest and relaxation. After a hot and satisfying meal, we went up to the hotel rooms to shower and change clothes. As I walked among the soldiers' rooms, I noticed that something had changed. The invincible expression in their eyes as we marched back into Israel had disappeared. As a commander, I knew that very soon we would have to go back to war and to more battles, and I tried to understand what was going on.

The answer was lying on top of the beds. Alongside packages of candy and snacks, new socks and uniforms, the headlines of the daily newspapers screamed "Sitting Ducks at Bint Jbeil" and "Unnecessary Battle," followed by descriptions of battles written by irresponsible journalists. How different were the headlines in the summer of 2014 during Operation Protective Edge, illustrating the sharp transition made by Israeli society and public opinion-makers. The feeling of cohesion among all sectors of society and the full backing given to IDF fighters to function, as implemented in the operation, marked an important milestone in the return to sanity of a society bent on survival.

*   *   *

As a soldier in the training course for Egoz Unit, after navigation in northern Israel.

The "Forgotten Ambush"– as commander near Bint Jbeil during the withdrawal from Lebanon in May 2000. I returned to the same place in July 2006.

*As team leader in Egoz Unit,
in conversation with a squad
commander at Golani Junction.*

*Next to Yasser Arafat's offices in
the Mukata'a, Ramallah, during
Operation Defensive Shield
(April 2002).*

*A commander's leadership challenge– as commander of the operational company Haruv Battalion, during a rapid trek in the Jordan Valley. "We worked very hard to succeed." (Photo: Amit Klein)*

*With Roi Klein, my friend and commander.*

*Completion of a battalion exercise on the Golan Heights, with all the battalion officers, a few weeks before the Second Lebanon War. Some did not return – Roi Klein, Amichai Merhavia and Alex Schwartzman.*

*Photo taken during the battle, from the north side of the olive grove.*

*The combat area and path the forces took during the battle at Bint Jbeil.*

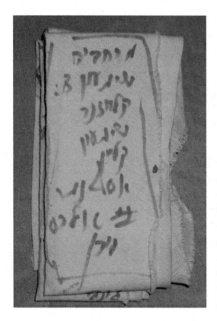

List of the casualties on a medic's personal bandage.
First Lieutenant Amichai Merhavia
Staff Sergeant Shimon Dahan
Staff Sergeant Ohad Klausner
Staff Sergeant Shimon Adega
Major Roi Klein
Staff Sergeant Asaf Namer
Captain Alex Schwartzman
Staff Sergeant Idan Cohen

Toward the end of the war, in a house near At-Tiri village in Lebanon. (Photo: Sagi Bakshi)

*Emotional meeting with Ma'ayan and the kids on the Lebanese border, after a few days of fighting.*

*This time in the reserves – meeting brothers-in-arms. Center: Yisrael Friedler. Right: Erez Alkabetz (July 2015).*

"For the sake of Zion I will not be silent, and for the sake of Jerusalem I will not rest, until her righteousness shines out like brilliance, and her salvation burns like a torch" (Isaiah 62:1). I stuffed a slip of paper with this verse into my ID tag holder on completion of the officers' training course. Thirteen years later, I read it on the Knesset podium.

The kids look on as I receive the rank of lieutenant colonel in the reserve forces from Major-General Eyal Zamir, commander of the Southern Command.

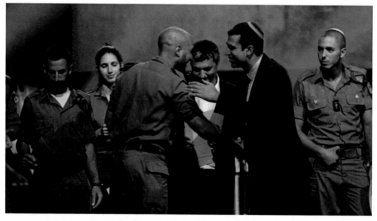

Appreciation event that I initiated for immigrant soldiers from France following Operation Protective Edge, this time as a member of Knesset (summer 2014).

We reached the moshav. The battalion officers had arrived at the shelter. Most of them had already painted their faces in camouflage colors. I went down the stairs, and on the wall opposite me I saw colorful children's drawings, meant to calm and cheer up the children in the shelter and add some brightness to the gray surroundings. Ever since the early 1970s, the residents of the north had been facing terrorist penetrations of their settlements and missiles shot at them from Lebanon – at first by the PLO, and later by the Amal and Hezbollah organizations.

As a little boy in Nahariya in the late seventies and early eighties, I have strong memories of the sirens and going down to the shelters. My mother, who had recently made aliya from France, was mostly alone, as my father was the physician on duty in the city hospital. My mother and I spent many hours together in the shelter. At that time in 2006, as always, the northern settlements were on the battlefront in the war to defend our home.

The officers' briefing was over, the sun was about to set. I found a little corner at the edge of the moshav and recited the Mincha (afternoon) service. I prayed hurriedly and without focus until I reached the concluding words of the silent Amida prayer, which succeeded in removing me from the surrounding reality:

> As for all those who plot evil against me, hasten to annul their counsel and frustrate their design. Let them be as chaff before the wind; let the angel of the Lord thrust them away. That Your beloved ones may be delivered, help with Your right hand and answer me. Do it for the sake of Your Name; do it for the sake of Your right hand; do it for the sake of Your Torah; do it for the sake of Your holiness. May the words of my mouth and the meditation of my heart be acceptable before You, Lord, my Strength and my Redeemer.

At 7:00 p.m., DBC Klein along with the deputy company commanders and battalion fighters went to the forest near the moshav.

The other officers and I went to meet them. In the seats on the bus, I saw soldiers painting each other's faces in green and brown camouflage, and checking their equipment. Some were deep in conversation with their mothers or girlfriends before they had to turn off their cellphones. We rode together to Moshav Avivim and reach the apple orchard next to the border fence. The night was very dark, as it was the end of the month of Tammuz and the moon was almost completely in shadow – perfect timing for an attack on foot under cover of darkness.

Hundreds of Golani Brigade fighters stood in enormous columns among the apple trees, carrying kitbags full of equipment and ammunition – a sight I'll never forget. The artillery forces began thunderous bombing of Bint Jbeil, and our war planes attacked targets in built-up areas.

This was it – the war had begun!

The engineering forces made a planned breach in the border fence and marked it with green fluorescent lights. Egoz fighters began to cross the fence, while we kneeled and waited for our turn, tensed and ready to move.

"Klein, do you remember?" I said to my friend the DBC, who came to the front of the line to time the battalion crossing.

"You mean that ambush just before the withdrawal?" he managed to answer me, before disappearing in his usual manner and continuing with his task without awaiting a reply.

I had just wanted to thank him, to express my gratitude for his insistence on landing a helicopter for us against all odds, and to get us out of Bint Jbeil, back in 2000. But I never managed to do it.

An electrifying feeling of power penetrated us all as we began to cross the fence. The engineering corps waved at us and slapped us on the back. We crossed the flat area at the edge of the moshav as a united force, and began to climb the ridge between Maroun a-Ras and Bint Jbeil. The sight was impressive. Artillery shells fell in front of us and accompanied us throughout the movement. In professional language, this was called a "rolling fire screen." Each shell that dropped illuminated the area for a few seconds, like a photographer using his flash.

We avoided the roads, as we suspected that Hezbollah would set explosives there. To avoid visibility against the skyline, we advanced two-thirds of the way up the ridge. The area was steep and rocky, and movement was difficult, especially with the heavy weight that the soldiers carried on their backs. We were not used to carrying such heavy weights. Years of combat and arrests in Judea and Samaria and the Gaza Strip meant that we no longer had basic skill. Several fighters slipped down the slope, and their comrades pulled them back up. First Lieutenant Amichai Mer-havia, platoon commander of the advance force in c Company, stumbled and fell a few yards down the rocky hill. His soldiers were worried, but he got up quickly and smiled. "See how important that helmet is! Lucky it's on my head."

After the war, the IDF changed its way of thinking, and beginning with basic training and throughout the training exercises, movement on foot was always done while carrying heavy kitbags and packs.

We reached the ridge. Across from us and below we could see the terrorist enclave of Bint Jbeil. The fire from artillery and the air force moved toward the built-up area. In the days leading up to the war, the IDF had dropped hundreds of thousands of leaflets from the air onto the town, calling the citizens to leave and distance themselves from the bloodthirsty Hezbollah terrorists.

We stopped for observation with the company commanders, to identify the territory and the buildings we were supposed to occupy. When I looked to the south and saw the carpet of lights coming from the northern Israeli towns I was filled with deep pride. We were fighting for our country, for its existence and honor.

We began to move north from the ridge into the built-up area.

Gradually and exactly as planned, the companies began to move rapidly through the streets to their targets. We took control of the buildings without any hitches. The Hezbollah were not aware of our entry into the town.

"This is Italy (A Company), Muki (code word for 'in position')."

"This is Givon (C Company), Muki."

"This is Hadassah (assisting company), Muki."

One after another, the company commanders reported over the radio that they had reached their targets and were positioned inside the buildings. The battalion commander and command post team, including myself, took up position in a building along with the assisting company. DBC Klein joined C Company.

In the top part of the building we were in, we set up machine gun and sniper positions. On the lower floor, we organized guard positions for the entrance and the combat squad and sniper zones.

"Forward! Put down the packs and set up a command table and maps for the battalion commander," I ordered the officers who were beside me. Our backs were completely soaked with sweat from the effort of the march. The straps of the packs left us painful souvenirs in the form of red stripes across our shoulders and necks.

Silence all around.

"Achhh," I groaned. I couldn't move – I had sprained my back. I couldn't believe this was happening to me. I really hadn't planned to start the war like this! How humiliating. I lay on the floor and had no choice but to inform Battalion Commander Asor that his operations officer was out of commission and needed a massage.

"Any volunteers?" Asor joked. Communications Officer Yehuda pressed on my back at a few points, and I writhed in pain. In the middle of my disgrace, Intelligence Officer Boji walked in and gave us his latest report: a terrorist cell was located inside the school next door to us, just a few yards away.

We identified the building on the code map and on the aerial photographs. The battalion commander authorized the brigade to shoot a missile at the building. We ordered all forces to go inside buildings and keep away from external walls to avoid injury from the shock waves.

"Yoni, you coming? Soon they'll be shooting close by," called Yehuda.

"The ceiling can fall in as far as I'm concerned, but I can't move," I replied.

Then we heard a deafening explosion next to the building, and the walls shook. After several long minutes, the pain subsided and I could function again. I tried to forget the embarrassing incident.

# Chapter 11

# *First Encounter with Hezbollah*

The operational concept of the division and brigade was to attack the enemy from several directions in a wide region, thus creating surprise and uncertainty. Hezbollah was unable to identify the source point of our attack. We got the impression that the Hezbollah fighters were wandering around the streets of Bint Jbeil, trying to figure out where the IDF was located and from which direction we had penetrated the town.

The Golani operations branch officer informed us that the paratrooper brigade had been delayed, and was stopped by the senior command due to concern that they would have to move in daylight. At that point, Bint Jbeil was surrounded on the east by Golani, while the paratroopers would complete the planned pincer maneuver from the west the next night – Monday, June 24, 2006.

"I told you so! Can't trust those paratroopers. I knew they would screw us over," the battalion communications officer commented in reaction to the report. I gave him a light kick to shut him up.

Then a volley of shots made us jump.

"This is Commander Italy. We have positive identification of three armed men. One killed, two ran off toward Hadassah."

The fighters of Rifle Company A had identified three terrorists. They killed one, while two others ran toward the location of the assisting company.

A second volley by the assisting company hit and killed another terrorist, but the third managed to flee. It all happened so quickly.

About an hour after this incident, Omer Niv, a gunner from C Company, identified another armed terrorist wearing a vest and carrying a Claymore mine. Niv shot a single bullet at the enemy, hit him in the forehead and killed him. On the first day of fighting, Golani was responsible for the deaths of some twenty Hezbollah fighters.

The term "fighters" is an appropriate term for Hezbollah activists. In encounters with the terror organization and when examining bodies after battle, it is obvious that their fighters are well-equipped and expertly trained. They wear military uniforms, wear bulletproof vests, carry cartridges and communications equipment, and are skilled at battle movement and operating explosives. Israeli culture has a tendency to belittle the enemy's abilities, but this approach is incorrect and can lead to unnecessary victims. Still, in every battle we find that IDF fighters are superior to Hezbollah fighters, who in most cases prefer to avoid contact with the IDF after they have been identified.

That night, a force under the command of DBC Klein moved toward the ridge to transfer intelligence material – maps and communications equipment taken from the terrorists' bodies – and returned early the next morning.

In the late afternoon of Tuesday, June 25, 2006, we received an order to retreat back to Israel. The forty-eight hours planned for the attack had ended. The fighters grumbled. The average combat soldier trains for months, even years for the opportunity to implement his skills and values of defending the country. Despite the disappointing feeling that the mission was over, the battalion commander ordered our forces to begin preparations for gradual departure from the buildings after dark.

My Mountain Rose satellite phone rang – Brigade Operations Officer Roi Levi was on the line.

"Tell Asor that we're staying."

The high command instructed the division to remain in Bint Jbeil. What was our mission? What were the goals? Everything was unclear. Throughout the night, the high command was unable to clarify orders for the division and the brigade. The confusion at the senior levels continued and left us standing there, stable in position, until we received a clearer mission.

Uncertainty is one of the most definite characteristics of the battlefield. This is an understandable reality in confrontation with the enemy. The enemy aims to surprise you. It wants to cause losses and disrupt your plan. But this time, the uncertainty came from the opposite direction – from within the military system. From inside.

We knew that we had succeeded in surprising the enemy. We had created uncertainty regarding the location of our forces, and the Hezbollah fighters were circling in confusion, like flies buzzing around at random. The indecisiveness in the senior command at that point in the fighting meant that we couldn't utilize the momentum we had created against the enemy.

We waited for orders.

*   *   *

Waiting in position is antithetical to the nature of the combat unit. Every commander at every level who has carried out an attack or maneuver in enemy territory knows that continuity of battle is the secret to victory. The enemy must feel at all points in time that he is being hit, and that he does not have the opportunity to reorganize. This is similar to a boxer who works with both fists simultaneously, striking first with the right and then the left, from below and then from the sides. This is the only way to force the enemy to surrender.

My positions in various battles have taught me that there are other factors that influence how decisions are made during war.

Consideration of international factors, public pressure, damage to the economy, and of course – the strength of the society. When combined, together these create the whole that leads to the best decision.

At the same time, political or military leadership that has already decided to go to war or to initiate a fierce battle against terror cannot stop midway. Immobility in battle or hesitation in the command ranks have a direct effect on efficiency and on the desired result for which the battle was initiated. In the background, this indecision also has a powerful effect on the soldiers and can hurt their morale.

*   *   *

In fact, at the senior command level, battles were taking place between the chief of staff and the commander of the Northern Command, and this affected the division under Hirsch's command. Quite possibly, the indecision at the senior levels and immobility were what enabled the Hezbollah to reorganize and eventually overcome our forces.

We moved into the depths of Bint Jbeil.

Around 2:00 a.m. we received the order to advance to the city center and improve our positions and take control over buildings that offered a better view of the surrounding area.

"Yoni, open the aerial photograph, quick!" ordered BC Asor. He marked the area of houses and the method of advancement: A Company would move first, with C Company behind it in stages. The assisting company would remain in place behind to provide cover. The forces rushed to get organized. The understanding then in place at all levels of the IDF was that no forces should move in built-up areas in the daytime due to the threat of anti-tank missiles.

"We have to finish before daylight," came the instruction. I looked at the faces of the platoon commanders and soldiers – the glint in their eyes had returned. The feeling was, "No one's stopping us! We're moving forward!"

Outside the fog was unusually dense. At 3:00 a.m. we moved

forward along with the battalion commander among the soldiers of A Company. The usual way to handle the fog was not exactly easy – each soldier placed one hand on the shoulder of the soldier marching next to him, and his other hand on his weapon. The commanders marched at the front and navigated using the aerial photograph that was updated in 2000.

I realized that the main threat was disruption within the force, meaning a soldier going the wrong way due to impaired view. The possibility of a soldier getting lost and disappearing in the fog worried me much more than an encounter with the Hezbollah.

One hour after we set out, C Company began to move toward their targets, along with DBC Roi Klein and Captain Itamar Katz, who had completed his position as company commander and had volunteered to join the battalion in this war. Previously, Itamar and I had both served as team leaders in Egoz. Katz had been the best friend of First Lieutenant Boaz Pomerantz, who had been killed alongside me in Operation Defensive Shield.

The built-up area around us looked like any ordinary town in southern Lebanon: two- and three-story houses with an olive grove surrounded by a wall, usually belonging to an extended family. Along with A Company and the deputy company commander, First Lieutenant Zafrir Tiferet, we took control as planned of an abandoned structure under construction. The heavy fog meant we couldn't see anything through the open windows in the building. Over the brigade communications network, we received reports that C Company was moving toward the three houses it was supposed to enter.

Although other military biographies of IDF commanders throughout Israel's history sometimes describe an unusual premonition that the enemy was approaching, one hour before the battle began, I felt no different than usual. I took out a dried salami and shared it with my comrades. I had no second sense of what was about to happen.

c Company was supposed to take control of three buildings – one for each platoon. Company Commander Alon had excellent platoon commanders under him: First Lieutenant Amichai Merhavia, advance force platoon commander; First Lieutenant Maoz Shabtai, patrol platoon commander; and First Lieutenant Shlomo Shuvi, explosives platoon commander, who arrived fresh from the officers course after a short training session in Gaza. For Shuvi, this was the first time he had served as platoon commander. The deputy company commander, First Lieutenant Alex Schwartzman, was a brave and professional officer. Like Alon, he had gone through Egoz Unit. Company Commander Alon Hachima had been a new recruit when I was commander of new recruits in Egoz.

A great company, no doubt about it.

## Chapter 12

# *"He Jumped on the Grenade"*

"This is deputy Barlev. We're at the staging area, over," reported Klein, who's with C Company.

The company commanders observed the houses and identified that they were in enemy-controlled territory. It's 4:30 a.m. We'd run out of time, and there were no better houses to serve as our operational base. Amichai Merhavia's advance company moved toward its designated building, which was surrounded by a high wall and an olive grove on two levels. Amichai and the advance force attempted unsuccessfully to break down the front door, while the other company fighters waited in the yard. Company Commander Alon realized that he was under pressure of time and decided to send the two other companies at intervals to take control of their two buildings.

At the battalion advance command post tensions were high as we waited for C Company to reach its targets. From the south, we heard shots and grenade explosions. C Company must have hit some terrorists, we thought. I grabbed the radio handset to ask for a report.

"Let them work. Don't bother them right now," said Battalion Commander Asor. The understanding of the command post was that C Company was exchanging fire with the enemy in the buildings they were supposed to enter, and that the encounter would end in a few minutes.

In the course of my military career, I have experienced many exchanges of fire with the enemy – some simple, some more complicated. Mostly they were quick and short. Usually, when the enemy is not regular army, such as terrorists, the battles don't last for long. Of course, we always aim to kill the terrorists as quickly as possible. But this time things were different.

Red (Eviatar Cohen), a machine gunner who stood next to the eastern wall around the yard of the house, identified an armed person who was looking at him. The person was not wearing a helmet. Then Hezbollah terrorists arrived on the scene from an unexpected direction. Red quickly regained his composure and began to fire. Klein threw a grenade and ordered the force to open fire and throw grenades.

The basic instinct of every IDF combat soldier is to stand up and charge. From basic training all the way through to the command courses, the cry of "Forward, charge!" is the immediate response that is expected from every IDF fighter. Ariel Sharon formulated this cry when he was a commander in the paratroopers, and it spread from there throughout all the IDF units.

But the wall in between prevented the C Company soldiers from charging, and the two sides began a grenade battle instead. Klein ordered Amichai to outflank the enemy from the right and neutralize them from a more advantageous angle. Amichai gave the order calmly. He climbed up to the upper olive grove and began the flanking maneuver with the advance force and Sergeant Shimon Dahan's squad.

"Forward, charge!" Merhavia ordered his team. From between the olive trees in the fog, the advance force didn't see that there was another wall in front of them, blocking their path. A terrorist cell lying in wait at the southeastern corner of the wall attacked them. Amichai was shot in the hand, then hit by a grenade.

"I'm wounded!" I heard Amichai's voice coming weakly over

the radio. Years later, I still remember the sound of his voice in those moments. I first met Amichai at a battalion training exercise on the Golan Heights. He was a platoon commander and I was the operations officer. The constant smile spread across his face hid a serious attitude and continuous concern for the welfare of his soldiers.

In a second, the entire area exploded – that was my first impression. Shooting broke out from all directions. The houses in the abandoned town came alive with firing from Hezbollah terrorists who began to shoot from the top floors. Dahan's force advanced and began to fire at the terrorists and simultaneously to tend to the wounded. The high wall obstructed shooting, and the fighters had to hold their weapons up high in order to fire over it. Then Dahan was fatally wounded by precise shooting and another grenade. The terrorist cell behind the wall on the right continued firing and throwing grenades at our forces. In retrospect, we learned that this cell caused a large number of wounded until it was destroyed, apparently at the initiative of Ohad Klausner and Alex Schwartzman.

At the battalion command post we realized that the encounter had become major. I heard the reports of wounded over the company communications network. At this stage at the command post, we were mainly trying to get an accurate picture of the situation. The location of the encounter was unclear. In a debriefing after the war was over, we learned that teams of drone controllers were in the air above us at the time, and they identified the location. Reports or directions from them would certainly have been useful, but for some reason we had received no information from them.

DBC Roi Klein heard Amichai's report on the radio and moved toward the wall with his own radio. He gave the order to continue firing and throwing grenades and disconnect from the area of destruction. Asaf Namer, who had insisted on leaving battalion headquarters and joining the company, returned fire from over the wall. Then a burst of fire came from the right and hit him in the head. He was killed instantly, falling on the ground beside his comrade Eviatar Turjeman, who kneeled down next to him.

A grenade landed in the middle of the force, falling next to Klein's legs. Klein shouted *Shema Yisrael* and threw himself on the grenade, absorbing the explosion and saving the lives of the soldiers around him.

"He jumped on the grenade! He jumped on the grenade!" shouted Shimon Adega, a fighter from the advance force.

Klein was gravely wounded. As a senior commander, the feeling of responsibility that characterized him in life was most clearly expressed in his final moments. With his last remaining strength, he gripped the handset and reported of himself, "Klein's dead. Klein's dead."

The battle continued. The fighters returned fire continuously and treated their wounded comrades. Ohad Klausner, the only one of Amichai's team not wounded bandaged the others.

We were in a building together with A Company, listening to their voices over the radio. In the battalion command post and the brigade operations room, we realized that the most urgent task was to get an updated status report. Without it, there was no way we could provide assistance and aim fire efficiently at the enemy that was hurting c Company.

At the beginning of the incident, the battalion commander ordered the A Company commander to advance. "Friedler, take a platoon to the front house. We must get a status report." Friedler prepared the patrol platoon to move to the front house to observe and assist c Company.

c Company Deputy Commander Alex Schwartzman and his communications officer Idan Cohen heard that Klein was wounded. Using an explosive brick, they finally managed to burst open the door of the building that had been designated for the advance force. They advanced through the olive grove toward the wall, but a terrorist cell at the corner of the wall shot a volley at them, wounding them both. Schwartzman was wounded in the right leg and fell down next to a tree. Cohen was seriously wounded. He was supposed to have been discharged in two weeks, but had volunteered to join the company despite back injuries.

"Idan, don't worry, we'll get out of here," Alex reassured him, kneeling next to him. Idan was evacuated to the advance forces' building by his comrades, but didn't survive his wounds.

The fighters who approached the wounded Schwartzman and Klein to evacuate them to the rear met with Schwartzman's obstinate refusal: "Get over to Merhavia – he's on the stretcher."

Shimon Adega and Eviatar of the advance force prepared to carry their commander Merhavia's stretcher. Then the enemy threw a grenade, and Adega was gravely wounded. Later on in the fighting, when I arrived at C Company's building to where the wounded and dead were evacuated, he lay bleeding on the living room floor. I'll never forget the look on his face. Our eyes met, and I smiled at him in encouragement. A few minutes later I went back to him, and this time his eyes were frozen.

The Adega family lives in Kiryat Gat. At age five, he had made aliya from Ethiopia along with his parents, siblings, and the rest of his family. Due to his health problems, the IDF refused to accept him into a combat position. But he insisted, fought within the army system and finally made it into the Golani Brigade. Each year on the memorial days, I meet his parents and his brothers, who also served in combat units. I'm frustrated by the fact that his parents can't communicate with their son's comrades and officers in Hebrew. The ability to share memories and talk about their son is part of the healing process, for the family and for us as well. When this can't happen, it's even more difficult.

The story of Shimon Adega's parents is similar to that of many other bereaved families in Israel. I think of the hundreds of thousands of soldiers and their families who made aliya to the country about which they dreamed and prayed. Most did not know Hebrew. For the many who were killed, their families were forced to deal with incomprehensible pain and loss in a foreign culture and language.

After Klein and the others fell, Company Commander Alon Hachima understood the difficult situation. He took a force from the patrol division, and together with Captain Itamar Katz carried out a flanking maneuver to the north on the road, with the goal of making contact with the terrorists. Heavy fire pounded his company from the house on the north. Platoon commander Shabtai Maoz shot a Lau missile at the building and silenced the source of the shooting. Then the force reached a barrier in the road, so they moved through the olive grove to the point of encounter.

Alon ordered his force to continue shooting. Then he ordered Shiran Amsili, the tall, broad MAG machine gunner, to jump on top of the wall and neutralize the terrorists. Amsili grabbed his machine gun, hurled himself onto the wall – thus completely exposing himself to fire – and began to fire furiously at the terrorists. For this heroic act and for treating the wounded under fire, Amsili was decorated with the commander-in-chief's citation.

But Golani remains Golani, and a few months later, his brave act didn't prevent him from leading a rebellion within the battalion against a new battalion commander...

Katz saw that Klein was still alive, and bound his leg with a tourniquet. With his remaining strength, Klein waved his hand and gave Katz the encrypted Mountain Rose phone device, ensuring that it wouldn't fall into enemy hands.

\* \* \*

I often think about my friend and commander Roi Klein, lying on the ground in Lebanon, losing blood after a supreme act of bravery. He was aware that those were his last minutes to live. I try to imagine his thoughts in those painful moments. Maybe he thought about his wife, Sara, and his sons Gilad and Yoav. Maybe he thought about all he had accomplished in his short life. But Klein was incapable of thinking only about himself. Klein knew that if the Mountain Rose phone device fell into Hezbollah hands, they could use that information against our forces, so he made sure to prevent this from happening.

*  *  *

To me, Klein, as we called him in the army, is not just the guy who jumped on the grenade. As I knew him personally, I am aware that his act of bravery is only the end of a meaningful life. My friend Roi Klein was a rare combination, gentle yet determined. On Yom Hazikaron before the war, we were both on active duty, Klein as DBC and myself as operations officer. At the formal ceremony held at Mitzpe Adi, Klein was asked to make a speech and light a torch.

"Yoni, please – you do it for me. I prefer to be an observer," he asked with his typical bashfulness. Often when I give speeches about the battle and I'm asked to describe my part in the fighting, I tell the audience that if Klein were there instead of me, he would probably be embarrassed and avoid talking about himself. Everyone who saw him with his children and family would never imagine that this was a daring officer from Egoz Unit of the Golani Brigade. He simply exuded gentleness.

Yet the soldiers and officers who knew him in battle and in the unit's operational routine were also witness to his ability to make resolute demands and set high standards. I was with him in my first encounter with terrorists as an officer and team leader near Nablus, where I witnessed him as a brave and fearless commander. The Sages relate that one of King David's names was "Gentle Lance" – when he was studying Torah, he made himself pliant like a worm, but when he went out to war, he hardened himself like a wooden lance (Babylonian Talmud, Tractate Mo'ed Katan 16b). King David, the daring commander of the Israelite army, knew how to act as gently as a lowly worm when not at war.

This was what Roi Klein was like for us. The Israeli combat

soldier, unlike those in other armies around the world (especially the professional ones), exhibits this same fascinating combination of fierceness in battle and gentleness in personal life. As one who lives in the world of the army reserves as a battalion commander, I can say that this is exactly what represents the human advantage of the IDF.

On my first day as a member of Knesset, I entered the well-known dining hall in the Knesset building and sat down beside a veteran Knesset member who had also served as a government minister.

"I have some advice for you, my young friend," he began. "In this place, you need to have the hide of an elephant and a heart of stone. That's the only way to make it," he insisted.

"Hide of an elephant – okay. Heart of stone – no way. I'll never give up my flesh and blood heart," I replied, remembering my commander, Roi Klein.

\* \* \*

Katz ordered the others to evacuate Klein. Three fighters began to carry his bleeding body. Yet another grenade hit Klein and ended his life. The young soldiers and squad commanders who had lost their senior commanders continued to fight and evacuate their wounded comrades to the building. Despite the shooting that continued from all directions, Ohad Klausner of the advance force continued to stand erect, calmly evacuating wounded, until a sniper's bullet hit his chest and he was killed on the spot.

# Chapter 13

## Rambam Under Fire

The encounter with the Hezbollah deteriorated.

When it started, I watched from the battalion command room as the A Company soldiers ran after Commander Friedler to a more distant building to help C Company. I noticed that one of the A Company squads remained behind, hesitating to advance. I realized that they had "missed the train." They were cut off from the rest of their company, and fire was coming at them from all around, preventing them from advancing along with the others.

"Asor, there's a squad here from A Company that's stuck in the rear. I'll lead and connect them up to Friedler's building," I informed Battalion Commander Yaniv Asor.

"Good luck," he replied.

Today, when I look back over the years, I realize that this moment and the way events unfolded afterward in the battle and the war had a profound influence on my life.

"Hi, my name's Yoni, I'm the battalion operations officer," I introduced myself to the surprised squad.

"Follow me and we'll get to the company building."

On the way to the building, we had to pass through a swath of open territory about ninety yards long (80 m).

"This is exactly the last thing we need right now," I think – crossing open land with no cover while bullets are being fired from all around is definitely a challenge.

"Do you remember the exercise for crossing enemy territory?" I shouted to the group of soldiers, whose names I didn't know.

"We'll cross one by one. I'll go first. When I lay on the ground and open fire, the next one after me moves. Let's go. Just like in training." I ordered the group to advance at intervals, which would reduce our exposure to the enemy. Continuous crossing together in a group would create a broader area for the enemy to hit.

I begin to run, lay flat on the ground and open fire. The next one after me moves forward.

"Excellent," I think.

In such a situation, the soldier's best friend is Mother Earth. Every protrusion or ditch that can provide cover is the best thing that can happen at that moment. We continued our advance. Another sprint, another jump, and I lay on the ground and begin shooting.

Suddenly a pile of dirt, sand and stones flew across my line of vision. A volley of three shots passed close to my nose – too close. Suddenly I realized that the next time I got up to jump, there was a good chance that the next volley would hit my body. At that moment, an image appeared in my mind – my wife Ma'ayan and the three children. I froze – I had to push that picture aside. As if my mind was an old-fashioned slide projector, I managed to insert a new slide into my thoughts. A completely different image appeared – on leave from the army, I went to visit the yeshiva I had attended, and sat with a group of friends to study together. A book of the Rambam (Maimonides) was set in front of us, open to his commentary on the book of Judges: "He should place his soul in his hands, and not fear or worry, or think about his wife or children. Instead, he should erase their memory from his mind and focus completely on the battle. Any individual who reflects on

war and frightens himself is transgressing a negative command-
ment, for as the verse says, 'Let your hearts not be faint; you shall
not be afraid, and you shall not be alarmed, and you shall not be
terrified because of them.'"

"Yoni, you're the commander. There are soldiers behind you.
Forward!" I encouraged myself. I got up and began to jump. I'm
certain that the Rambam saved my life in that moment. I have no
idea how long that "experience" continued, but even years later,
I am able to describe in detail the stages of my thoughts, feelings,
deep within my soul. In battle or in extreme situations under fire,
the concept of time becomes completely confused. In conversation with soldiers and friends after this battle, I discovered that
events we thought lasted for a few seconds in fact extended over
many minutes, and the opposite was also true – a continuum of
events that lasted for hours seemed to take just several minutes.

*    *    *

I learned a great deal about my life from this short incident. My
investment of time in study and examination of the values that
guide me as a person are a significant factor in explaining my
behavior. These values have a practical consequence in unexpected situations, especially extreme incidents when we have to
focus all of our abilities. Israeli society is an amazing variety of
people who have gathered together to establish a state. Naturally,
there are sharp differences of opinion about the moral base that
leads us as a society and a people. Shared discussion and clarification as a family or society are vital in shaping our future.

*    *    *

We crossed the open area safely and reached the front house,
which was occupied by A Company. Over the radio I heard later
that Alon Hachima, commander of C Company, was also severely
wounded. Captain Itamar Katz declared that he was taking command, and ordered his troops to cut off contact from the "destruction area" in the olive grove and move toward the company's

protected house. In a rapid calculation, I realized that almost the entire chain of command in c Company was wounded or dead.

A Company Commander Friedler and I go up to the top floor of the house to find a good angle of vision from which we could observe the battle. Our main mission was to understand what was going on. This was the purpose of reaching the front house.

We found a wide window facing west toward the encounter. Friedler clung to the wall on the right side of the window, and I was on the left. The terrorists were still shooting, and we had to avoid exposure in order to prevent additional wounded.

Daylight came, and we saw soldiers running all around, shooting and throwing grenades. It was hard to distinguish the c Company soldiers from the Hezbollah. The terrorists wore olive green uniforms and bullet-proof vests, and carried weapons, and from a distance, they looked the same as IDF soldiers.

Boom! I heard a single loud shot from up close. I knew what it was – sniper fire. Friedler flew backwards and lay on the floor. The situation looked like a scene from a Western film. I saw that a bullet had entered his elbow and flew out the other side. In the pocket of my uniform pants, I carried a bandage. I threw it at him, and two soldiers nearby jumped on top of him and applied the bandage. Friedler held the communications handset and continued to give orders as if nothing had happened.

"Chetboun, bro', I'll kill you if you tell anyone that I'm wounded," Friedler warned me. There was no time to digest this or to be surprised. The voices of c Company coming over the radio revealed that the situation was bad.

## Chapter 14
## *A Fateful Decision*

I go back to the window and lift a pair of binoculars. I see soldiers carrying wounded comrades to the house. I see the wall and the two central houses from which Hezbollah fighters are firing. Over the radio, I hear Avichai Ya'akov.

"Our ammunition is gone. Again, our ammunition is gone. We need help. Over."

Avichai, a brave and resourceful squad commander, realized that most of the command chain above him was wounded. He entered the olive grove to evacuate the wounded and dead. He went in and out of the field six times, giving orders and encouraging the other soldiers with fighting spirit. For this outstanding performance in battle Avichai was awarded the medal of courage.

The voices of the commanders shouting over the radio, the shooting and the wounded reminded me of the reports of the brave commanders at the Suez Canal in the Yom Kippur War. Several weeks earlier, during the training exercise on the Golan Heights, I had finished reading the biography of Ariel (Arik) Sharon. The chapter that describes the dialogue between Commander Sharon and the soldiers at the positions under Egyptian attack left a deep impression on me. In those moments at Bint Jbeil, I felt everything rising up within me.

"I have to get to them," an inner voice called.

Again, I tried to get an overall picture of the situation. Two relatively high buildings overlooked the olive grove and the surrounding area from the east – one gray, the other white. The terrorists and most of the shooting was coming from that direction. I surveyed the territory in all directions, my brain working at the speed of light.

Then I made my decision. I would outflank the enemy from the north in a wide circle, and reach the c Company battle area from behind. The movement was dangerous, but the area looked relatively quiet. I trusted my analysis of the area and my experience as a commander in battle, and I knew that this was the right thing to do.

"Friedler, I'm taking the squad that came with me and going out toward c Company. They need help over there," I reported to the wounded A Company commander.

"You're nuts."

I ran down the staircase to organize the force that would come with me.

"c Company needs us. Almost all the commanders have been wounded. We're going on an outflanking maneuver and then we'll connect with them," I updated the soldiers from the A Company squad. I had no time to learn their names. I gave out count-off numbers – there are six of us including myself.

In a normal situation, in another time or perhaps in another army, I would have expected harsh resistance. But it was quiet, as everyone understood the great need.

I informed the battalion commander over the network, and coordinated my approach from the north with Itamar Katz, who had taken command of c Company.

I ordered the force how to advance. "We'll move forward using the same method as before. I'll jump first, and you all come after me one by one. Don't fire if you don't have to. I don't want the enemy to discover our path. Good luck!"

We start out and move in leaps as planned, on a slope between agricultural terraces. I look back at the group. We had gone through so much in a short time, and I had no idea what their names were. The sound of shooting continued from the battle area. The entire battalion was involved in the battle against the terrorists, Rifle Company A and the assisting company, each one in its own sector.

### RETREAT OR CONTINUE?

Even in war you can find yourself in particularly embarrassing situations. That's what happened to me just several dozen yards after we set out for the C Company battle area.

"Yoni, I can't move my leg!" shouted one of the soldiers from behind. I rushed to the rear and saw a soldier lying on the ground motionless. I was sure that he had a bullet wound. But after checking his leg, I couldn't find any bullet entry or exit hole.

"Your leg is fine. You have to keep moving!" I shouted at him.

"Yoni, my leg is stuck. I can't move," he insisted.

I lost my patience. This really wasn't the time for a soldier to be frightened into inaction.

"I don't give a damn! Get moving. Your friends over there are wounded!" I screamed at him, shaking him furiously. But nothing worked. He didn't move.

After the war we learned that this soldier, Eliran Biton, had in fact suffered a gunshot wound. A bullet had grazed his leg and hit a nerve, and his leg was paralyzed. After the battles, I apologized to him for doubting his reliability. He forgave me, a true Golanchik. But the embarrassment didn't end there.

What should we do? We were just six soldiers all together. Should we continue to advance and leave Eliran in the field, along with another soldier as back-up? Should we go back? Maybe I took too great a risk?

No book or guide can give fixed solutions for any situation.

Decision-making is the greatest challenge of any commander. Within minutes, as when I was standing in the window of the house before deciding to move, I had to make yet another decision, to combine my entire value system and professional experience together with risk management and clear-headed thinking.

"We're moving the wounded soldier back to the house with another soldier, and the four other soldiers will continue to advance," I inform the squad. I order Nir Meltzky, a young squad commander (whose name I didn't know at the time), to carry Eliran back to the house using the "one on one" method for carrying a wounded soldier.

"Do I look like I'm going back?" said Meltzky, surprising me. "I'm continuing on with you into battle. Tell Assis the sergeant to take him," he insisted.

Elad Assis, an experienced sergeant, reacted angrily. "Tell that young squad commander to take him. I'm moving forward with you."

There in a Lebanese olive grove, I found myself in the midst of a rare, irrational argument between two stubborn Golani soldiers. It was incredible – they weren't arguing about who would go home for a long weekend, but rather who would march into fire to fight. In that situation, I could either laugh or cry, but again I had to decide.

"The sergeant has a radio. He can report his retreat," Meltzky said decisively, making the winning argument. The return to the house had to be coordinated with the other forces, so that our forces wouldn't shoot at them by mistake. I ordered the sergeant, who made sure to show me that he was not happy with the decision, to evacuate Eliran back to the house at the rear.

After the battle, I met Sergeant Assis. He smiled at me as he reminded me of the incident. "Remember you sent me back. So you should know that thanks to you, I killed six of the terrorists."

While the fighting continued and c Company pressured the

terrorists to retreat, Elad Assis had identified seven of them from the window of the bathroom in the house. He shot them in the back and killed six of them – every infantry soldier's dream.

I continued the deep outflanking maneuver along with three fighters: Meltzky, Sani Agbaba and Yiftach Caspi. The entire time, Itamar Katz and I spoke to each other on the company communications network. There was a significant risk that a soldier unaware of our movement might fire at us.

Next to the northern building from which the terrorists had shot at Company Commander Alon Hachima in his outflanking attempt, I identified a Hezbollah missile launcher. It was placed among the olive trees, with a cache of missiles beside it, and aimed at Israel. I had the uncontrolled desire to stop everything and take care of it myself. Based on the map, I reported its exact position to the battalion commander. After the battle was over, the brigade destroyed the launcher.

We approached the area of houses assigned to c Company. I was pleased that we had succeeded in finding a hidden approach route at the enemy front, and I believed that we could bring in additional forces that way.

"Katz, this is Yoni, over," I got on the radio to Itamar who had taken command, to coordinate joining up with them. We used our first names instead of the usual radio communications code, as we were officers who didn't belong to the force in an integral manner.

We climbed up the patrol platoon's building. Suddenly I saw an M16 aimed at me from the door.

"Hold your fire! It's the operations officer!" shouted one of the fighters to Dudu Sabag, who was standing in the doorway and hadn't received the report of my arrival. I had a fleeting thought of how horrible it would have been if Sabag had opened fire at us...

\* \* \*

On the annual memorial day of the battle at Bint Jbeil (1 Av) in 2015, I returned late at night to my home in Jerusalem from the settlement of Eli. The memorial for Amichai Merhavia had just ended, and as I was driving home, my cellphone rang. Dudu Sabag and Yisrael Ben Lulu from the patrol platoon, who had fought with me in the battle, were on the phone.

"We wanted to tell you something important. You've probably heard about it," they began, starting the conversation in a serious tone. "Remember when Sabag almost shot at you?"

"Of course," I replied.

"So the same thing almost happened to me," Yisrael related. "I saw you approaching us with your troops. I was next to the wall in the olive grove, and I aimed my weapon at you. I was sure that you guys were terrorists attacking us from another direction. To this day I don't know why, but I stopped myself from shooting at you. I just had to tell you that now. I kept it to myself for a long time, but now you know," he concluded.

"That's just fine, bro," I replied.

"We're here together. We have a mission to continue telling the story of our friends who fell in the battle."

The next day, as I do every year, I held a small celebration of thanks in the synagogue after the morning service. This time, after my conversation with Ben Lulu, I felt the need to say a double thanks to God.

\*   \*   \*

At the door I met Avichai Ya'akov, who gave me a sincere smile. "Thanks for coming, we've been waiting for you." In his eyes, I could see the difficult images he had witnessed in the past few hours in battle. Afterward, I heard that during one of Avichai's sorties to evacuate the wounded, he saw Alex Schwartzman, the deputy company commander who was wounded in the leg and refused to be evacuated. Avichai dragged Alex back, but a volley shot from afar hit Alex in the chest, and he died in Avichai's arms.

Avichai led us to the advance force building. In the doorway I met Itamar Katz, who had taken over command of the company after Hachima was wounded. Realizing that the olive grove was "destruction territory," he was calmly ordering evacuation of the wounded to the building. We hugged each other.

"What's up, bro'?" I asked.

"Could be better," replied Katz with his cynical sense of humor. I entered the living room, which was enveloped in the pungent smell of blood. The memory of odors is particularly powerful, and to this day, I can smell that horrible stench. The wounded lay on the floor, neatly sorted according to level of wound by Eran Eliyahu, company medic. It was absolutely silent. No one groaned, even though they were in pain. Some had grenade shrapnel all over their bodies, the others had gunshot wounds.

After the war, the wounded related that before he died, Idan Cohen lifted their spirits and gave them hope that they would get out of there alive.

I opened the door to a side room and saw the bodies of the dead that were evacuated to the building. They had not yet been covered with blankets. Katz was operating correctly. He had placed the casualties in a closed room, thus maintaining the soldiers' morale.

Then I went up to the top floor. A squad from the *hesder* yeshiva (combined army service and yeshiva studies) platoon was shooting at the terrorists and the buildings that were targeting the olive grove. Beside each fighter I saw another weapon – that had belonged to a fallen comrade. The cover force on the top floor hit and killed every terrorist who moved close to the location. They were doing excellent work.

The arrival of our new force put smiles on the faces of the fighters and their commanders and gave them new energy. The feeling that they were cut off from the rest of the battalion in a deteriorating situation was gradually reversed.

We had to win.

In the review conducted after the battle, many of the fighters emphasized the fact that welcoming a fresh force from outside in the middle of battle was more significant than the operational activity and the shooting we initiated to destroy the enemy.

"Yoni, there are five more guys lying in the grove next to the wall. It looks like they're already dead," Katz reported. "Klein's there, too. It's really hard to evacuate them from there because of the shooting," he added.

There's no way they're staying there, I said to myself.

As one who had taken over command of a company and of commanders he didn't know previously, Katz quickly realized that we had to get an updated status report of names and numbers of wounded and dead. The threat of kidnapping a soldier was a central component of this war – that was how the whole thing started.

At an early stage, he placed a force under the command of Yoni Jano outside the building to cover the grove and guard the dead bodies from being kidnapped. The force was in danger, as it was exposed outside the building and firing constantly. The sniper, Sasha (Alex Sirenko), stood outside shooting non-stop and hitting terrorists. An automatic grenade-launcher hit his position, but he recovered and continued shooting at the Hezbollah, even though he temporarily lost his hearing.

It was almost 8:00 a.m., and the shooting continued constantly. As operations officer, I recalled the possibility of air assistance with combat helicopters. "Where are they, damn it," I mumbled to myself. I realized that until then, due to the close encounter between our soldiers and the Hezbollah, our air forces were unable to open fire. The risk of friendly fire due to lack of information about the exact location of our forces and the enemy prevented them from becoming involved in the battle.

Battalion Commander Asor came on the radio and informed me that battle helicopters with the signal code "Crush Dance" would soon contact me to coordinate. He defined my code name as "Yoni's Force." On the staircase I met Elad Ozeri, Roi Klein's communications officer. I noticed a blue smoke bomb peeking out of his vest pocket – excellent.

"Ozeri, from now on you're my communications officer. Come with me." We went up to the roof of the building.

"Hey, Yoni, this is Crush Dance. What's going up?" I hear the helicopter pilot calling me over the radio. His slow speech and easygoing manner annoyed me. Hey, I felt like telling him, there's a war going on here. In retrospect, though, it was very helpful. For us infantry men who were in the midst of the inferno and rapid pace of the battle, the calm tone of voice of an outside entity helped lower the stress level.

"Yoni here, I hear you," I answered.

"You sound five-five," he continued in his slow, steady voice, using the air force expression for "very good."

"Yoni here. I'm going up on the roof and I'll send up a blue smoke bomb for you. Over."

Ozeri and I race up to the middle of the roof and throw the smoke bomb. The helicopter pilot identifies us. "You're at location xxyy." Everyone who has ever navigated knows the feeling – there's nothing like the feeling you have when you're in the middle of a solo navigation on a dark night, and you meet a comrade at a shared point. It gives you confidence. That's how I felt when I realized that the pilot knew where we were.

"Yoni here. Accept our force's line. You're close to fire from the wall of the olive grove and westward," I specified the location of our force, feeling confident of my ability to direct a battle helicopter. The knowledge and experience I had accumulated along with my comrades in dozens of training exercises and operations, particularly in Lebanon, enabled me to do so. There's no substitute for training and experience, I reminded myself throughout my service, and this was true for the reserves as well.

The two structures on the east, gray and white, kept nagging at me, because the terrorists were using them as their base for most of the shooting and attacks. I directed the helicopter toward them. One missile, another missile – I identified a hit. The damage is slight, but the explosion created a shock effect and a short silence ensued.

"We have to exploit the shooting to remove the dead from the grove," I said to Katz. He went up to the top floor and asked for volunteers to go into the olive grove with me. It wasn't easy – the grove was traumatic territory for all who had fought there. Katz glanced at Vlad Kazetchkov, a squad commander from the patrol company who had temporarily lost his hearing from the shooting. Vlad joined me and Shlomo Shuvi, commander of the explosives company. Katz and I planned to place a cover force on the top floor and another one at the entrance to the grove, to guard Shuvi, Vlad and myself while we evacuated the dead. We gathered the fighters on the level of the living room, where the wounded still lay, to give out orders and tasks. I looked straight into their eyes, and most of them looked straight back. The accursed olive grove was enemy territory. They had witnessed as their comrades were wounded and killed there. Most of the shooting was directed there, and now we had to go back there. On the other hand, it was clear to each of us that we couldn't leave any soldier in enemy territory.

The cover forces took up their positions on the top floor and at the entrance to the grove. There was a new, strange feeling of tension. The method I had chosen was to have a combat helicopter shoot a missile as the forces opened fire. Then the three of us would race into the grove.

We ran. The first and closest to us were Company Commander Amichai Merhavia, who was on a stretcher, and Sergeant Shimon Dahan. One after another, we carried Amichai and Shimon back to the house. It wasn't easy, as a steep terrace stood in our way. We had to do it quickly, but our desire to preserve our dead friends' honor slowed us down.

Once again, we opened fire while racing into the grove. After the war, Vlad described his feelings during those moments. "I'm a lone soldier, as my mother lives in Canada. The army doesn't have the phone number of any of my relatives – not my mother, not my father, not even my grandmother with whom I was living. If I died, who would let my family know? But after I saw Shuvi and Yoni get up, I knew that I had to go, too."

On our third entry, we reached Deputy Company Commander Alex Schwartzman, who had refused to be evacuated, and then was fatally wounded while Avichai was dragging him.

We go in a fourth time. Next to the wall I lift Asaf Namer and carry him back. In a flash, I recall the conversation we had in the Gaza Strip and his insistence to go back into combat. On our fifth entry, the combat helicopter opens fire. Under cover of the fighters' fire as well, we race to pull out Roi Klein. The sight was gruesome, but cold logic prevented emotions from interfering with the task we had set ourselves.

The evacuation stage ended. All of the dead and wounded were taken out. My throat was dry from the effort, and I desperately wanted to drink all the water I was carrying, but I knew that the battle wasn't over and I had to save it for later.

To carry out final verification of the wounded and dead, Itamar Katz instructed medic Yehiav Levi to write on his "triangle" (a triangle-shaped bandage for binding sprains) the names of all the fighters and their status. Katz himself performed the job of identifying the casualties, in a closed room.

\* \* \*

I often think about the great privilege I had to be there in the olive grove in Bint Jbeil. My fallen comrades lay on the ground in their olive green uniforms, a representative sample of Israeli society. A human mosaic of the people's army.

Ohad Klausner was from Beit Horon, a community settlement on the road to Jerusalem. His parents lived and breathed Zionism. They were among the founders of the settlement, in which secular and religious Jews lived together. Shimon Dahan of Ashdod was from a family of Moroccan immigrants who exuded warmth and loved welcoming guests in their home. Asaf Namer's family had moved from Israel to Australia, but at age twenty-five, he chose to volunteer for combat service. Shimon Adega had made aliya from Ethiopia, and despite his medical problems, he made it into Golani. Alex Schwartzman, who made aliya from the Ukraine, had lost his father at age fourteen. Although in the Soviet Union his family's connection to Judaism was almost non-existent, his mother insisted that his gravestone bear the inscription: "Descendant of the dynasty of the Ba'al Shem Tov." Idan Cohen of Jaffa insisted on joining the battle despite his health condition, and was killed two weeks before his discharge date.

Neighbors of Amichai Merhavia of Eli in the Binyamin district wrote that he was from a family of pioneers in Judea and Samaria. His parents helped found the settlement of Ofra. Roi Klein grew up in Ra'anana and raised his family in Eli. He was a commander with a love of books.

To me, and for many others in Israeli society, the IDF is a Zionist reserve, an institution that preserves values of dedication and commitment to state and society. It may be the only entity in the State of Israel where a citizen declares, albeit silently, from the moment he puts on a uniform, that he is willing to give up what he holds most dear on behalf of a value greater than himself.

From its establishment, Israel has faced a series of security challenges on many fronts. The motivation of the IDF soldiers that we witness in all Israel's battles stems from the fact that it is a people's army. The ability to create a consensus around the uniform, with the participation of citizens of many varied opinions on the political right and left, immigrants and long-time residents, religious and secular, is what enables the army to win and defeat the enemy, even in times of crisis. The Yom Kippur War, which involved dozens of heroic battles like Bint Jbeil, is a perfect example of the ability of a people's army to rise above the mistakes of its leaders.

I do not deny the fact the people's army model also creates tensions and deep divisions within society. The question of drafting the ultra-Orthodox arises every few years and causes eruptions within the political system. But today it is clear that we cannot make social changes with threats and force, particularly changes that have never before been made, ever since the establishment of the state. Such changes must take place out of dialogue that respects others and their values, and of course recognizes the fact that the State of Israel draws its values from Jewish faith and heritage.

*   *   *

The ability of the air force to identify our forces and open fire against the enemy was very significant for us. Those who were severely wounded needed immediate evacuation. We had to reduce the amount of enemy fire in order that rescue forces could move toward us on foot. In the division of roles between Itamar Katz and myself, we decided that Itamar would continue commanding the company, while I would be responsible for the shooting and directing the rescue forces that would come to meet us by moving along the access route I had established.

In coordination with Battalion Commander Asor, we decided that the engineering company, under the command of Erez Alkabetz, would join up with us on foot to help evacuate the wounded. We had been together in the officers' training course. Erez was a composed and highly professional officer who had proved his command abilities in dozens of operations and extreme situations. I was very pleased when he joined us.

"Yoni, this is Deputy Meridor, over." On the radio I heard a well-known voice in a heavy Brazilian accent that sounded exactly like Yisrael Friedler, A Company commander. The last time we were together he was wounded by a bullet in the elbow, and as I recalled, his radio code name was Italy Commander. In fact, it turned out to be Yisrael's brother Dani Friedler, deputy commander of the Golani engineering company, who had come to us for preliminary evacuation of the wounded. Their family had made aliya from Brazil when they were young. All of their children had chosen combat service and had gone through the commanders' course. For me, this was like closing a small loop in the battle.

I directed the engineering company fighters to the outflanking route I had taken a few hours earlier. The encounter with Erez, Dani and the other engineering fighters who arrived with stretchers, medical equipment and ammunition was the best expression of the IDF's spirit of comradeship. Quickly and efficiently, the engineering soldiers loaded the most severely wounded onto stretchers and began to move rapidly to the A Company building. From there the wounded were evacuated to the helicopter landing point by patrol company fighters under the command of Major Shai Kelfer.

The complicated and dangerous evacuation operation was directed by Battalion Commander Asor, who coordinated the movements and the simultaneous firing at the enemy. Some twenty soldiers with various levels of injuries were transported from the C Company sector in three rounds. The evacuation mission ended around 3:00 p.m. We decided to take out the casualties at night so as not to endanger the evacuation forces. The stage of deciding who is most severely injured and must be evacuated first is a complex professional challenge for the medics. My stubbornness almost caused the death of my friend Alon Hachima, the injured company commander. While the wounded were being prepared for evacuation, I noticed Alon standing up and leaning against the stairway railing. At first glance, I saw no signs of injury on his body.

"Take Hachima out in the next round," I instructed Eran Eliyahu, company medic.

"No way! His wound is severe. I'm the medic and I decide. Yoni, believe me, I'm right." I was angry, but I had no time to argue. I went back to coordinate the shooting and direct the air forces to assist in evacuating and neutralizing the enemy. In fact, Alon was the most severely wounded soldier who survived the battle of Bint Jbeil.

Throughout the battle, the company and battalion fighters hit the Hezbollah from several different directions. The force on the upper level of the house kept up the shooting ceaselessly and hit a large number of terrorists. The enemy began to retreat, and after the company managed to focus fire efficiently, they were hit by the assisting company and A Company with the support of air forces.

Around 4:00 p.m., silence fell. Actually, it was a "noisy silence" – the firing almost completely stopped, but my mind was buzzing. Eleven hours of continuous fighting from 5:00 a.m. finally ended. I was exhausted. The hunger and thirst that I had pushed aside reminded me that I was merely human. I knew that the soldiers felt the same way, but we couldn't let down the level of operational tension then. The situation could turn around at any second. The casualties were still with us in the room next door, and we had to prepare to take them out under cover of darkness.

The quiet outside was similar to the silence within the house. The soldiers who weren't guarding the openings of the house sat quietly on the floor in all corners and on the staircase. Katz and I moved among them. This group of young soldiers and squad commanders, the vast majority of whom were experiencing battle for the first time, succeeded in turning the situation around and winning the battle. After most of the officers were hit and the command chain fell apart in the early stages of battle, these soldiers took initiative, fought and evacuated their comrades.

"Can you hear me?" I asked Vlad, making funny movements with my hands. The guys laughed. Vlad had lost his hearing in the battle, but slowly he began to regain it. He smiled and realized that he was the object of his friends' laughter.

I went over to the staircase and sat down. "Yoni, I can't move," said the soldier sitting next to me.

"What's the deal, bro'?"

"My body's stuck, I'm, like, paralyzed," he explained.

One of the medics examines him and reports that he doesn't see any wound. I recalled how the soldier had acted in battle – he had moved around, evacuating wounded and helping to send them out after the engineering corps arrived. I hadn't noticed that he was physically wounded. I got on the Mountain Rose handset to speak to the battalion commander, who was in the A Company sector, and I told him that we had another wounded man.

"I'd like to talk to him," Asor requested. I listened to their conversation – a warm dialogue between commander and soldier after battle. Slowly I realized what Asor had known right away – the soldier was suffering from battle shock.

"Hug him, and try to keep talking to him. Keep him beside you," said Asor. Slowly the soldier was able to sit up and then walk.

I learned a lot from that incident. A commander in a combat unit is required to lead soldiers under fire. He must act professionally and he must win. At the same time, understanding the emotional workings of a soldier and how how he performs and reacts in extreme situations is a vital component of the commander's abilities. The military system must provide the commander with professional tools so that he can identify such conditions at an early stage.

Darkness fell – it was 8:30 p.m. I searched for volunteers to come with me to the olive grove again to collect the battle equipment that remained in the field. Platoon Commander Shlomo Shuvi and Dean Schuster came with me. Yiftach Caspi and Vlad Kazetchkov volunteered to cover our movements. I was equipped with night-vision equipment, as outside it was completely dark –

and quiet, the exact opposite of what we had experienced in the last hours of the battle. We collected bullet-proof vests, grenades and battle equipment that had fallen off the casualties and wounded as they were evacuated.

Two engineering company teams and a platoon from Rifle Company A came to the building to carry out the eight soldiers who fell in the battle at Bint Jbeil. The column of soldiers carrying their comrades, who lay on stretchers covered with blankets, moved on foot to the A Company building. Battalion 12 training company under the command of Captain Zafrir Bar-Or, which had come to deliver supplies and food, carried the stretchers over the ridge between Jabel Khil and Maroun a-Ras. This was also the stage when Company Commander Yisrael Friedler finally agreed to be evacuated, after being hit in the elbow at the beginning of the battle.

Eight years later, I participated as a Knesset representative in the funeral of Major Zafrir Bar-Or, who was killed in the Gaza Strip during Operation Protective Edge. Zafrir had served as deputy commander of the Golani patrol battalion.

The soldiers of the training company under the command of Captain Gal Karabaky carried the dead to the Achzarit transport vehicles, and from there they moved to the border fence. One of the platoon commanders who helped load the stretchers, including the one with Amichai Merhavia, was his good friend First Lieutenant Asahel Lubotsky. Several days later Asahel was severely wounded in the legs near Bint Jbeil.

# Chapter 15

## *"While We're Here, No One Shoots at Families in the North"*

Meanwhile, in Israel, things were noisy. That day, Ma'ayan and the kids went to my parents' house in Netanya and they went to the beach. It was summer vacation, and Daddy hadn't been home for too many weeks. All afternoon, battle and rescue helicopters flew over their heads, moving north along the beach.

"Yoni's in the operations room. He's not a company commander any more, so he's not supposed to be on the front line," said Ma'ayan to my parents, attempting to placate them. My father had been a flight physician in the reserves, and he realized that something big was happening on the northern border.

Slowly, rumors about the fierce battle of Battalion 51 reached my family.

"Is everything all right?" asked a close acquaintance, who held a senior position in the IDF, on the phone to my father.

Ma'ayan felt dizzy. She expected to hear the worst. In the evening, she and the children went back to our home in Jerusalem. If bad news comes, it'll be better for the kids to be in bed in their warm beds, she thought.

Later that night, after we finished evacuating the wounded and the dead, Shimrit, an officer in the battalion operations room, called to give Ma'ayan an update about the results of the battle, and let her know that I was fine.

I often think about the bereaved parents and the wives and children of my comrades, who received a different message. The question of "Why them and not me" is often at the front of my mind, but above all, there's another question that bothers me – how to make my life meaningful after it was given to me anew as a gift at Bint Jbeil. I am very sorry that not everyone was granted that privilege.

To enable the air force to bomb Hezbollah missile launchers and other war materiel that were identified during the battle, we returned on foot and took up position in the A Company building. For the first time since the battle had begun, I took off my battle vest and equipment. I had to stretch my body a bit and get some air after the sweaty effort. I looked at my uniform – it was stained with my comrades' blood. But as opposed to what one might expect, I felt a powerful feeling of pride for the honor I had been awarded, despite the pain.

Inside the building, I found a little bathroom with running water, and I washed off the blood. I didn't want the other fighters to see me like that. We still had an entire war ahead of us.

I made the rounds of the soldiers. To me, these were the Lions of Bint Jbeil. The atmosphere was tense, with some turning inward to reflect, others talking about the battle. I felt something volatile in the air. Again we were waiting in position without a defined mission, but it seemed that the momentum of battle was not yet over. Standing still in the heart of enemy territory also creates a feeling of irrelevance, of "what are we doing here."

"In five minutes, everyone come into the left-side room," I informed the fighters. I realized that the time had come to talk and explain. Silence in the room.

"What's going on?" I asked the soldiers, who were crowded

together on the floor. "Bring me the marker from my vest, please," I asked one of the medics. On the wall of the room, I drew a map of the State of Israel and its northern border. One by one, I marked Kiryat Shemona, Metulla, Zefat, Hadera and Haifa.

"We are here," I said, indicating a point on the map inside Lebanon. "While we're here, no one can shoot at the families in northern Israel. No one shoots from Bint Jbeil at our kids and mothers. Thanks to you and our comrades who fell in the battle, thousands of men and women can feel safe. No one knows how long this war will last. But one thing is clear to all – it's better for us soldiers to be on the front, and not families and children.

"And one more thing," I had to add. "I truly love and admire you very much."

Sometimes I wonder whether my Israeli work of art is still on the wall in that Shi'ite town in Lebanon.

A day passes while we wait in place.

Then Battalion Commander Asor updates me: "Tonight we're going back to Israel." It's Friday night of 4 Av, June 28, 2006. The long battalion column begins to march toward Israel and the border fence. This was a column of straight-backed combat soldiers who had fought in battle. The results of the battle were clear – despite the painful losses we suffered, we defeated the Hezbollah at Bint Jbeil. During the battle, we killed some forty terrorists of the Hezbollah "special force." Together with the results of the air strikes, intelligence estimated that the organization's losses totaled around one hundred men. From the almost impossible position in which c Company found itself in enemy-controlled territory, the situation was transformed thanks to the bravery, determination and solidarity of young soldiers and commanders, and despite the fact that the chain of command was almost entirely shattered.

Mainly, we felt that we had fought and carried out what was expected of us as combat soldiers in the Israel Defense Forces. For us, the war as we had experienced it until then was a victory.

* * *

We stopped the family car in the parking lot behind the Yokneam mall. Herut, Shilo and Emunah were sitting in the back seat. Herut and Shilo were old enough to understand that there were bad people who wanted to harm their country, and that's why Daddy had to go back to the army.

The driver Lazry was waiting for me in a military vehicle to drive me to the battalion before our next foray into Lebanon.

"Promise me you'll come back, God willing," Ma'ayan asked. I looked at her and at our children. It was hard for me to say good-bye – my heart was overflowing with love and worry, and mainly with thanks that I was still alive.

"Promise. I feel like I still haven't finished my mission in life," I answered her with inexplicable confidence.

Today I know. My brothers-in-arms and I, the ones who are still alive, must continue to tell our story. We must share with as many as possible the message of the greatness and power within us as a people. The strength of this people in its infinite variety reaches its ultimate expression in the soldiers of the IDF who are prepared to give their lives for the State of Israel.

# Afterword

Despite the time that has passed and the operations since then, such as Operation Protective Edge, the battle at Bint Jbeil still draws the interest of people who represent a wide range of ages, opinions and worldviews. In recent years, since the Second Lebanon War, I have lectured about this period and its significance in many forums and sectors of the Israeli public.

"What moment in the battle was most difficult for you?" This is a question I often hear, after I finish describing the fighting among the olive groves in Bint Jbeil. My answer usually comes as a surprise to the audience.

The usual expectation is that the close encounter with death and the feeling of being under enemy fire are a faithful expression of the hardest moments of battle. Certainly, a good answer to this question is the fear of being wounded, the horrible images of comrades wounded and killed, grenade explosions, voices of soldiers calling for help over the radio, and the shots whizzing close by.

But actually, for me the most difficult moment was at a completely different point in time. While under fire in the face of the enemy, and especially in a command position, the soldier pushes images of battle aside. Your brain and emotional and physical resources are all focused on one goal: success of the tasks required in those moments. In this situation, the human body has a fascinating mechanism that does not permit fear, doubt or shocking images to get in the way.

In talking with friends and other fighters after the war, most describe this phenomenon. Of course, after a while the brain processes the events – the images and odors of battle become deeply engraved in our memory. The most difficult moment that I remember was actually the moment before – the seconds when I had to make a decision. There in the window of the house we occupied, hundreds of yards from the shooting and the mayhem of battle, I looked through the binoculars at the C Company soldiers as they fought the Hezbollah terrorists. I heard the voices of the squad commanders as they called over the radio for help and the grenade explosions, and I realized that the chain of command had been almost entirely shattered.

Ostensibly, the cement walls of the building we occupied and the distance from the site where I was likely to be wounded were the best thing for me at that moment – I felt safe. But I asked myself to make a decision – the question burned within me. Do I remain in the safe space, or do I dare to move out into the chaos, when no one expected or ordered me to do so? This moment was the hardest for me, even harder than the battle and commanding under fire.

Even now, as I write these words, I can feel the terrible uncertainty – whether to take the risk and endanger others along with myself in the uncertainty of the battlefield. That moment in the window in Bint Jbeil is carved into my soul – I will take it with me for the rest of my life.

Making decisions in life is a daily challenge in our personal lives, not just in battle. At almost every moment, we have to choose between good and evil, and between good and better. Human nature mostly tempts us to remain in the "safe house," in our comfort zone. Many of us are frightened by the idea of entering that door of uncertainty. Although there are moments when reality demands that an individual make a change in his life, the fear of change can influence him to stay in place.

This understanding hit me once again, one month after the war. At that time, I was battalion commander at a post on Mt. Hermon, carrying out operational duties on Israel's cold border, with silence and long hours at guard posts and on patrol. The daily routine started to get to me, and I felt disturbed.

"Where is the power and the energy that pushed you to make decisions and act tirelessly in battle?" I asked myself. As time goes on, the more I understand that the biggest challenges are not just in Bint Jbeil while under enemy fire, but in the gray areas of daily life. Many times in life we are required to leave the comfort zones to which we are accustomed, focus our strength and make decisions that can transform us and those around us into better people. I recall my comrades who fought beside me, the young soldiers and commanders who decided not to accept reality as it was, and I know that it's possible. It's certainly not a simple task, but when we complete it, our lives take on a deeper meaning.

At the same time, we must clarify the sources of strength that enable us to make the right decision. This is what I did.

At that moment in the window of the safe house, before making the decision to lead fighters into the fray and join the battle, I had to draw strength from those sources. Looking deeply, I identify three sources of strength that assisted me, and I believe that they are relevant for anyone who wants to make choices regarding the dilemmas he faces in life.

## SOURCE I: LEARNING FROM OTHERS

In Bint Jbeil, the voice over the radio of Squad Commander Avichai Ya'akov, calling urgently for assistance and reporting that "Our ammunition is gone," reminded me of the situation of the brave soldiers in the Yom Kippur War. Shortly before the Second Lebanon War, I read the biography of Major-General Ariel Sharon.

His description of the soldiers' cries over the radio on the banks of the Suez Canal, under attack by the Egyptian army, made a deep impression on me. During the battle in Lebanon, this impression was the most immediate factor in my decision to go out and assist.

To my mind, learning from others' experience as a result of reading, learning and in-depth analysis or shared discussion is the first and most readily available source of strength that a decision-maker can use.

## SOURCE 2: THE POSITION – COMMITMENT FIRST

When a person is a commander and officer in the army, this gives him the responsibility to do whatever he can to carry out the task he is given and to guard the safety of his soldiers. The commitment to the IDF ethical code, which emphasizes the value of devotion to the task alongside preserving human life, becomes an inseparable part of the commander. In the decision I had to make, this component was significant, although in the war I served as operations officer and was not required to do so. In battle, I often said to myself, "Yoni, you're a commander! Get moving!"

The commitments that we take upon ourselves in various fields force us to stay involved. They make us act and respond toward those around us. Whether consciously or not, the position leads us to take responsibility. Society and state must encourage and develop individuals who volunteer to take responsibility in many areas, who will be the first to act when reality demands it.

## SOURCE 3: VALUES

A volley of shots passed close to my head as I led the force, and I froze in place. At that moment, I thought of my wife and kids. Then I had a flashback to studying the Rambam, who wrote about the fear of war in *Yad Hachazakah*: "He should not fear or worry, or think about his wife or children."

When my soldiers advanced behind me and watched to see what their commander would do, I thought of the biblical judge Gideon, who said to the Israelite fighters, "Watch me and do as I do" (Judges 7:17). In those moments, the entire range of values I grew up with rose up inside me.

Values are the most significant of the sources in this list. The value system that a person brings with him to the decision-making moment has a dramatic influence on its character, quality and correctness. The range of populations and opinions in Israeli society is broad, and, of course, each individual's value system is made up of many components. Despite our differences, we cannot ignore the fact that individual attention to ethical consciousness creates responsibility. Over the years, in my mandatory army service and in the reserves, I have noticed that what unites us as a people is greater than what divides us.

\* \* \*

As a society, we also must repeatedly ask ourselves – What are the sources of our strength as a people? What are the factors that give us the ability to make appropriate and correct decisions? Of course, this clarification is all the more relevant for anyone who chooses to make a commitment and become a partner in social or public leadership.

Today, Israeli society is in a fascinating period of its history. The question of our social identity as a nation and as individuals occupies us more than ever. This is a natural process comparable to human life. In his early years, the child is mostly concerned with his basic needs: nourishment, warmth, physical contact. Then as the child grows older and becomes an adolescent, he begins to ask the questions that define his identity and values.

As a society, Israel is now at the stage of adolescence. As we reach the completion of this stage, we must begin to find answers to these questions, despite the challenge they involve. I am opti-

mistic. The encounter with Israeli society in its broad variety
in the IDF, in regular service and the reserves, exposes the firm
base of values on which we stand. This base enables us to stride
confidently into the future.

# Acknowledgments

I would like to thank my commanders throughout my military service, both regular and reserves, from whom I learned valuable lessons about leadership and military professionality. I also thank my brothers-in-arms and my soldiers – for the shared marches over the roads, through riverbeds, over plains and on top of ridges, through the vistas of our homeland and outside it, on behalf of Israel's security.

To the parents, the brothers and sisters, and the children who lost their most precious ones – thank you for allowing me to feel like family with each and every one of you.

To Moshe Merhavia for the assistance and details of the battle at Bint Jbeil – thanks for the encouragement and warm words about the importance of publishing this book.

To my friend Dr. Asahel Lubotsky, a man of letters and action, for the shared thinking and good advice late at night.

To Yair Ansbacher, for giving me tools when I took my first steps.

To Ayelet Zur, for the assistance in writing clearly and concisely.

To my wonderful editor Maya Bertal, who took on the project of editing on a tight deadline, out of her boundless love for the IDF and commitment to the stories of the fallen soldiers. Thank you for your true cooperation, enthusiasm, and efficient and professional work.

A special thanks goes to my friend Dov Eichenwald, CEO of Yediot Aharonot Publishing, for his good will and faith that this book was worthy of a place on the bookstore shelves. To Eyal Dadush, Vice President of Yediot Publishing, for the strategic thinking and giving me confidence.

On the publication of the English translation, I would like to thank the staff of Gefen Publishing for their quality and personal support, and for giving me motivation to publish the book for the English-speaking world. This is also the opportunity to thank a very special person, Mr. Ilan Greenfield, owner of Gefen, a Zionist and lover of Israel through and through.

In the process of translation into English, I was privileged to get to know Jessica Setbon, an outstanding and highly professional translator. Translating a book is not an easy process for the author, due to the very real fear that the messages might be changed or the personal style corrupted. With her years of experience and special sensitivity, Jessica transformed the translation process into a very positive one for me.

A most heartfelt thanks goes to my friend and lover of the Jewish people Mr. Meir (Mark) Blisko, who assisted me greatly and dedicated this edition in memory of his dear parents, may their memories be blessed.

Last but not least, I thank my family. To my parents, thank you for implanting within me and my siblings the values of Zionism, love of the land and the state. You have always served as my example and ideal in my personal and family life. To my brother Yair, for his constructive comments and words of encouragement.

To my dear children – thank you for your patience, interest and constant encouragement while I wrote this book.

And to my beloved wife Ma'ayan, for the shared journey replete with challenge and significance, and for serving as an anchor of stability in the challenging times of my military service and public life. Without you, this book would never have been published. Thank you for the encouragement and for understanding that I needed to write and bring to light the events that I experienced during my service.

I thank the Creator of the Universe for enabling me to return from the inferno, alive and well.